T0326306

Claiming Agency

Reflecting on TrustAfrica's first decade

Claiming Agency

Reflecting on TrustAfrica's first decade

Edited by

Halima Mahomed and Elizabeth Coleman

Published by TrustAfrica
Senegal and Zimbabwe
and
Weaver Press
Box A1922, Avondale, Harare,
Zimbabwe
2016

Typeset by Weaver Press, Harare
Cover Design by Xealos
Printed by Directory Publishers, Bulawayo

ISBN: 978-0-7974-73-881 TrustAfrica (p/b)
ISBN: 978-1-77922-301- 2 Weaver Press (p/b)
ISBN: 978-1-77922-302 - 9 Weaver Press (ebook)

Contents

Contributors

Hakima Abbas is trained in political science and international affairs. Her work as a policy analyst, trainer, strategist, and researcher has focused on strengthening and supporting African movements for change. She is a member of the *Jang!* popular education collective, is the editor and author of several publications and is on the editorial collective of *The Feminist Wire*. She is currently Director of Programs at AWID, a global feminist organisation, and serves as a board member to Greenpeace Africa and the Rosa Luxemburg Foundation Eastern Africa.

Alice L. Brown is an attorney with extensive experience in social justice philanthropy and public interest law. She advises, speaks, conducts research and writes on topics including philanthropic giving, leadership development, organisational effectiveness, and transformation in the South African legal profession. Amongst other pursuits Ms Brown also convenes the annual Public Interest Law Gathering and serves on the boards of Section27, Corruption Watch and Keystone Accountability. For nearly 20 years, she served in various leadership positions with the Ford Foundation, last as Southern Africa Representative based in Johannesburg.

Elizabeth Coleman is a writer and editor who specialises in philanthropy and social justice issues. She worked for 15 years for the Ford Foundation, first as a consultant then on staff as managing editor. As an independent consultant in Dakar and now Geneva, her clients have included TrustAfrica, the Open Society Initiative for West Africa, several United Nations agencies, and organisations focusing on women's rights, human rights and people-centred development.

Halima Mahomed is an independent consultant whose work focuses on research and advocacy to strengthen the narrative, knowledge, practice and impact of African philanthropy. Over the last 15 years she has been closely affiliated with, amongst others, the Ford Foundation, TrustAfrica and the Global Fund for Community Foundations. She is also a member of the Working Group on Philanthropy for Social Justice and Peace and of the Alliance Magazine Editorial Board. Halima has written extensively on African philanthropy. She holds a Masters in Development Studies, with a focus on social justice philanthropy.

Bhekinkosi Moyo writes widely on African philanthropy. He is currently the chief executive officer of the Southern Africa Trust and Chair of the African Philanthropy Network. He also serves on the African Union Foundation Council and on the Board of the International Society for Third Sector Research.

Chipo Plaxedes Mubaya holds a PhD in Development Studies from the University of the Free State, South Africa. She is Deputy Director/Senior Research Fellow in the Directorate of Research and Resource Mobilisation at the Chinhoyi University of Technology, Zimbabwe. Chipo worked with the African Climate Change Fellowship Programme from 2010 to 2013 at the Institute of Resource Assessment, University of Dar es Salaam. Her research interests are in rural development, agriculture and natural resource management and rural and urban climate change adaptation.

Tendai Murisa holds a Doctorate in sociology from Rhodes University in South Africa. He has published journal articles and book chapters and has co-edited a number of books. His research interests have mostly focused on rural development, social mobilisation and civic agency. He is a practitioner interested in ensuring the development of policy processes that contribute towards socio-economic justice on the continent. Murisa is the executive director of TrustAfrica.

Fambai Ngirande is an activist and international development practitioner based in Harare who works extensively with progressive groups to secure social and economic justice, human rights and democratisation in Southern Africa. His major interests are in movement building, public policy and research. Over the past 10 years, Fambai has been involved in formulating and implementing citizen-driven campaigns and initiatives across a wide range of issues such as illicit financial flows, climate change and corruption.

Humphrey Sipalla is a freelance consultant and adjunct faculty at Strathmore University Law School in Nairobi. He also serves as managing editor for the *Strathmore Law Journal* and edits for Strathmore University Press. Between 2010 and 2013, he served as the founding editor of the African Human Rights Caselaw Analyser, a trilingual database of the decisions of all African continental and regional human rights bodies of judicial and quasi-judicial character. Humphrey attended the UN Mandated University for Peace and Kenyatta University.

Preface

Sometime last year, in a conversation on the value add of having African institutions disburse funds that have originated outside the continent, I was asked: *Why African philanthropy? What makes TrustAfrica more than just a fiscal intermediary?* In response, reflecting on what I saw as the value add of the institution beyond its ability to disburse funds; I recall thinking about the written evidence for this, and knew that we fell short in this regard.

A few months later, TrustAfrica was approaching its 10th anniversary and wanted to explore how it might do three things: (i) undertake an interrogative and critical reflection that would help the philanthropy and development sector better understand the nature of its approach; (ii) celebrate the work that TrustAfrica, together with its partners, had been able to achieve and contribute towards, while simultaneously learning from its blind spots and challenges; and (iii) contribute towards an evidence-based body of knowledge and inquiry that would help advance the agenda for African philanthropy. And so the idea of a book was born.

With African philanthropy increasingly coming of age and with a growing body of theoretical and conceptual writing, but not enough evidence-based knowledge interrogating its value, I knew this book represented a moment whose time had come. Developing this concept with TrustAfrica's Executive Director, Tendai Murisa, and my co-editor, Elizabeth Coleman, we immediately agreed that a praise book of TrustAfrica's accomplishments would not serve any larger purpose, nor would it be fruitful for our own learning. We also knew that an overall evaluation, while certainly useful for the institution, would not really have relevance for, or contribute towards, discussion and debate in the field more broadly. We thus decided on a publication that would interrogate TrustAfrica's work from the perspective of two themes that lie at its roots: African agency, and the belief in the potential of African philanthropy to do things differently.

We knew that we wanted a rigorous examination of the work; we also knew that this would mean letting go of some of the powers we had to craft a narrative, and so we invited independent authors to examine some of our key programme areas, through a combination of TrustAfrica documents and interviews with TrustAfrica's staff, donors and funded partners, asking them very specifically to interrogate TrustAfrica's work – both the positives and negatives – and draw out the lessons learned.

We must note here, that although this book looks at the work of six particular programme areas, there are many others. TrustAfrica, for instance, has also made a significant input towards supporting education, looking at both early learning and higher education. In fact, TrustAfrica hosted alongside others, one of the biggest continental summits on higher education in 2015. TrustAfrica has also worked to nurture the development of small to medium scale enterprises through its ICBE Research Fund. The six areas in the book, however, provide a broad reflection of the nature of the type of work undertaken by TrustAfrica. We should also note that while one of TrustAfrica's three core focus areas is philanthropy, we have not included a specific chapter on that, and have sought instead to use it as a lens through which to view the overarching exploration.

While this book is a reflection on TrustAfrica in particular, we see TrustAfrica as one of a set of like-minded African institutions which, despite receiving funds from the global north, are committed to leading with African agendas – and so we hope that this book will provide a learning agenda not just for TrustAfrica, but for the many who support, fund or work for foundations in Africa.

* * *

While this is a book about TrustAfrica as a philanthropy institution that aims to mediate resources – fiscal and otherwise – towards a more just society, we are but one cog in the wheel; the programme achievements are a testament to the cumulative efforts of the hundreds of partners on the ground who are working every day to address these critical challenges, in what are fluid and challenging contexts.

TrustAfrica is also indebted to its donors – to the Ford Foundation and its staff for forging ahead and enabling this idea of a multi-programme pan-African foundation to become a reality, and to the many other donors who have worked and continue to work with us in our efforts to help forge a different development path.

The work of TrustAfrica would not have been possible without the anchoring and direction of its founding Executive Director, Akwasi Aidoo, its Board (both former and present members) and the dedication of the staff who have been, over the years, such valuable flag bearers for the potential of this institution and the realisation of its aims.

Elizabeth and I would like to thank the authors who agreed to take on this task; their contributions provide a rich and expansive window into TrustAfrica's work, the key programmatic issues at hand, and the practice of African philanthropy. We thank TrustAfrica's programme staff for the many chapter reviews and feedback, and its Executive Director, Tendai Murisa, for the freedom to pursue this independent reflection. We are indebted to Kepta Ombati, who served as the external reviewer, and whose contribution was invaluable in helping to shape the thoughts and ideas in this book more cogently.

Lastly, we acknowledge the support of our loved ones; we are indebted to their patience with our endless deadlines. Editing a publication of this nature, within the timeframe we had, has been a challenging effort, but one so well worth it.

Halima Mahomed

1

African Agency at Work

Halima Mahomed and Elizabeth Coleman

'There's a dignity in influencing your own destiny.'[1]

The topic of African philanthropy might strike some as abstract. But very real images rise from the pages of this book. In Ghana, a smallholder farmer influences her nation's agriculture policies. In Liberia, advocates work with officials to make resource extraction more transparent and beneficial to communities. At the African Union, activist researchers advance a new initiative to stem illicit flows of money from the continent. These are just three examples of work supported by TrustAfrica, one of the continent's few multi-programme, pan-African philanthropic institutions. If you factor in the multitude of similar actions that the foundation has supported over the course of a decade, you get a palpable sense of African agency – people across the continent who have taken it upon themselves to deepen democracy and promote the kind of economic development that benefits all people.

It was with this in mind – the belief in and capacity of Africans to make their own choices about their future – that TrustAfrica was established. What began in 2001 as the Special Initiative for Africa incubated at the Ford Foundation in New York, became, in 2006, an independent, pan-African foundation based in Dakar. Today, with a focus on three

---

1   Theo Sowa, the CEO of the African Women's Development Fund, in Sowa (2013).

overarching thematic areas – governance, equitable development and African philanthropy – TrustAfrica has, through partnerships with and resourcing from a range of donors, made more than 500 grants worth over $25 million, reaching more than 300 organisations in all regions of Africa and the diaspora.[2]

The idea of TrustAfrica was seeded at a time when, despite several years of democratic progress and a new wave of optimism about the continent and the potential for its leadership, power was once more becoming concentrated in elites. In many places, governance was moving further away from its mandate to serve all people and the objective of economic growth was superseding that of social justice, resulting in a rise in inequality. Increasingly, African people across the continent were finding themselves without much say in the decisions that would affect their lives – decisions that were, in many cases, being made by the new political and business elites, whose priorities did not necessarily match those of the continent's citizens at large.

In terms of resourcing, this was also the era of international development aid, but despite the billions of dollars flowing to the continent, the aid system too had failed to address the systemic challenges inhibiting Africa's progress. Part of the problem has been that those disbursing the aid often control the agenda[3] – whether it originates from private sources, bilateral and multilateral agreements or international finance institutions. Moreover, a major portion of international aid for Africa was (and still is) routed through global north or international non-governmental organisations that then decide where and how that aid should be spent on the continent.[4] Given these dynamics, solutions to Africa's challenges were often developed outside its contexts. Whilst some gains were certainly achieved, by and large, international aid fell far short of the transformative promises it had made.

This was a time when the role of civil society would be critical to holding governments to account on their mandates, to ensuring that the interests of citizens were paramount in key governance decision-making

2   This excludes funds directly spent on research, convenings and technical support. And it is over and above the initial $5 million that was distributed under the auspices of the Special Initiative for Africa.

3   See Tendai Murisa's discussion in Chapter 8 of the structural flaws of bilateral and multilateral aid agreements.

4   In Chapter 2, Bhekinkosi Moyo writes that currently more than 75% of U.S. foundation funding to Africa is administered by intermediary organisations headquartered outside Africa.

processes and to ensuring that development priorities were informed by those most affected. But the kind of civil society organisations that would take forward such a role required the independence to do so – independence of resources, independence of action and independence of priorities and solutions. It was thought that such independence could best be gained through the philanthropic sector.

TrustAfrica came into this context as an African philanthropic institution committed to enabling African solutions to the continent's challenges. The strategic entry point for its work was to support an independent civil society to advance its own priorities and craft its own solutions. From its first days, TrustAfrica set out to do things differently, and its founders had a conviction that TrustAfrica would represent something that was alternative to the norm. Indeed, the *TrustAfrica Chronicle* quotes Tade Aina,[5] reflecting a key element behind the institution as '…the desire and motive to establish an independent African-led foundation focused on engaging Africans in Africa and the diaspora in creating solutions together' (Barya and Richardson, 2012). Moreover, based on the continent, with a staff and board comprising individuals who themselves were active in Africa's development processes, the new foundation saw the potential of having a frontline view that would enable it to tap into and leverage the unique opportunities available for African agency to address the development challenges facing Africa.

TrustAfrica thus saw its work grounded in a collaborative approach with civil society and, from inception, held that the institution would listen to and create the space for African thought leaders to debate pressing issues and help set the agenda for TrustAfrica's programmes. Murisa, in his chapter, reflects this as a core role of acting as both 'a catalyst and collaborator' that would foster dialogue and strengthen civil society to claim democratic space. This was critical: the work would not just benefit people, but include them.

Given these founding values, this book reflects on whether and how TrustAfrica has indeed done things differently over the course of the last ten years. It interrogates the extent to which its work counters the mainstream philanthropic approach and if that way of working enables a different trajectory of impact for those who bear the brunt of Africa's social justice challenges. Does its work, in fact, enable a different agen-

---

5   Tade was a Ford Foundation Representative intimately involved in the founding discussions that led to the establishment of TrustAfrica, and later served as one of its founding Board members.

da? The book further interrogates the implications for the foundation's future work and for institutionalised African philanthropy.

Why this book now?

TrustAfrica has always recognised that its work, together with that of other like-minded African philanthropies,[6] represented a somewhat alternative approach to the norm, and has recognised the need to be ever-mindful of how it is undertaking its work and vigilant that it stays true to its course. To this end it has engaged in several learning endeavours; as the work of TrustAfrica and its partners has taken root across the continent, its work and impact has been documented in institutional reviews, programme evaluations and other publications. This book, however, is different. With TrustAfrica's 10th anniversary coming up, it sought to explore a slightly different learning agenda than previous reviews – an agenda that allowed for the application of a critical and interrogative lens through which to examine the premises underlying TrustAfrica and see how it has fared against them; and whether in fact those premises have had the intended impacts.

Accordingly, at the ten-year mark, with a decade of work in hand, TrustAfrica reached out to five independent authors to each undertake an external reflection on the evolution of particular areas of programming. Its mandate to these authors was to interrogate TrustAfrica's work under the concepts of African philanthropy and African agency, using a combination of primary internal documents as well as interviews with TrustAfrica staff, donors and funded partners.[7] The brief called not for an overall internal evaluation, but a specific reflection from these two angles, in the hope that collectively it would begin to tell us the story of TrustAfrica's approach. Finally, in the spirit of being open to critical reflection and constructive criticism, the authors were encouraged to examine the challenges, limitations and blind spots that emerged in TrustAfrica's work – in the hope that it would enable TrustAfrica both to learn and to provide broader lessons for the sector. The brief to the authors was one of independent review; the findings were their own.

Hence five chapters of this peer-reviewed book look at the institu-

6 For instance, the Southern Africa Trust, the African Women's Development Fund, the Kenya Community Development Foundation, and Akiba Uhaki.

7 TrustAfrica deliberately chooses to see those it funds as 'partners' and not 'grantees'. For TrustAfrica, the former term denotes more appropriately the nature of the collaborative relationships at hand, while the latter is often seen to denote a fiscal relationship only.

tion's contributions to strengthening a particular ecosystem or civil society initiative(s) intent on resolving critical democracy and development issues in Africa. Two additional chapters, by former and current staff, address the bigger picture; one surveys the history and potential of the fast-growing field of African philanthropy, and the other draws lessons from the other chapters to discuss how TrustAfrica and institutional philanthropy as a whole can build effective movements to advance social change.

While the occasion of the 10th anniversary provided the opportune moment to examine its work, there was another underlying, much more pressing reason to undertake this book. Now, even more than when TrustAfrica was founded, we are witnessing increasing threats to the independence of civil society. These threats come in many forms – from a narrowing regulatory environment for civil society, to restrictions in the nature of the activities civil society can undertake, restrictions in amounts of foreign philanthropy and the voluntary withdrawal of private funding. These threats affect, in particular, civil society organisations which are working to address systemic challenges and advance social justice; by the very nature of their work, they are often challenging government and holding it to account. Such work, in Africa, is not easily resourced.

A different kind of philanthropy

Lately, the African development sector has been pinning its hopes on an expanded philanthropic arena – especially emergent African high net worth individuals – who, it is hoped, will play a role in enabling a more independent, vibrant and sustainable civil society. While institutional philanthropy in Africa has indeed increased, with some exceptions most of it is not directed at addressing the systemic issues that drive injustice, focusing instead on more ameliorative and reactive responses to injustice. Now, more than ever, is the time for the rise of a different kind of institutionalised philanthropy, and this book hopes to reflect the potential role of that kind of philanthropy – while still being mindful of its challenges and limitations, particularly in regard to African philanthropic institutions that derive funding from outside the continent.

African philanthropy, in its different forms, has long played an important role on the continent. As Bhekinkosi Moyo explains in Chapter 2, philanthropy has deep roots in Africa and has served as a key vehicle for social cohesion in contexts where people have been oppressed and marginalised. Any discussion of the field must thus recognise its links to notions of solidarity and mutuality, and this extends to the current proliferation of institutionalised philanthropy as well. This institutionalised space includes private, corporate, family and community-based institutions as well as public foundations such as TrustAfrica, the African Women's Development Fund, and the Southern Africa Trust. This book reflects on the potential for a distinct role for African philanthropic institutions, not just because they represent development decisions and resource allocations being made on the continent, but because of the potential they hold to focus the power of their resources and freedom of decision-making on addressing the structural or systemic causes of injustice and inequality.

Addressing systemic issues, however, requires challenging the status quo, and facing head-on the issue of power (including speaking truth to power as Tendai Murisa posits in Chapter 8). Indeed, at a time when development resources are shrinking, Moyo envisions the field's potential to use its leverage with governments 'to reclaim local agency for civil society [and] reform restrictive laws'. However, collaborating with government can be difficult terrain. If it is to support the transformation of power relations between elites and ordinary people, the sector must keep the issue of power front and center. Moyo reminds us that as 'a constitutive part of civil society', philanthropy is and should be directly linked to its struggles.

Power, agency and African money

> We all have power, different types of power. When we don't acknowledge that power, it's easier for others to step all over us. .... We're not good at talking about power, and because we don't talk about it, we don't learn to use it well (Sowa, 2015).

For civil society, true power plays out in the form of agency, loosely translated as the belief in and capacity of people to make their own decisions. In Chapter 3, Humphrey Sipalla surveys how the discourse on African agency has changed over time, from the cultural pride of the Negritude movement in the 1920s and the wave of political independence in the 1960s to today's focus on accountability advocacy in which people are driving their own solutions and holding those in government as well as other duty-bearers to account. Enabling this requires, as Sipalla goes on to say: 'centralised African decision makers be humble enough to allow knowledge to flow from the local and the periphery to the centre'. In Chapter 6, Chipo Mubaya anchors the concept of agency in the academic literature of sociology and community development, which sees 'farmers' actions transcending specific planned technical behaviours on farms to performing roles as members of social networks and collectivities'. She contends that this view of farmers' 'creative capacities to respond to both socioeconomic and environmental shocks' is very much at the centre of the efforts by TrustAfrica and its partners that are enabling farmers to have a say in policy changes that boost their productivity and improve their livelihoods.

Why is it important to promote African agency? Yao Graham of Third World Network has said: 'If you don't have clarity of your own agency, you become someone else's project'[8]. Broadly speaking, this has been the case with Africa's development agenda, which has long been shaped by the priorities and views of Western donors. Indeed, this outsourcing of the continent's development challenges, as Fambai Ngirande puts it in Chapter 5, is what gave rise to TrustAfrica's focus on African agency as core driver of solutions. This is further emphasised by Hakima Abbas, who writes in Chapter 7, 'Given that resources yield agenda-setting power, their distribution cannot be dictated by people or entities removed from the continent and with multiple interests that may or may not align with African peoples.'

At the same time, it is still true that most funding for social justice work emanates from outside the continent. Is it possible to programme the distribution of these external funds in a way that nevertheless fosters African agency? In a context where civil society is under threat, and where foreign funded institutions are being labelled as imperialist agents (see Murisa's chapter), how do we separate the issue of agency from the geographic source of funds? Which begs the question: Is African philanthropy about the *source* of resources or the *control* of resources irrespective of the source?

In Chapter 8, Murisa reflects on TrustAfrica's experience to emphasise that the geographical source of the funds is not the ultimate enabler – or dis-enabler – of agency. Sipalla too, interrogates the notion of whether one can nurture African agency without spending African money, and his chapter reflects well how foreign funds enabled rather than distorted TrustAfrica's agency, and in turn the agency that was supported on the ground. At a time when international criminal justice efforts

---

8   Graham said this at the Power Panel at the AGN Assembly in 2012. As cited in Mahomed and Moyo (2013).

in Africa were being vilified as imperialist, TrustAfrica and its partners were able to build an authentic African response by supporting processes based on and led by the continent, and by bringing victims' voices to the fore. Sipalla concludes that the fact that donors have an agenda 'does not necessarily mean that they act to the detriment of African agency'; in essence, it depends on how that agenda aligns with local priorities and how flexible that agenda is to being changed as needed. Similarly, Fambai Ngirande's chapter on work to stem illicit financial flows (IFFs) from Africa shows how funds initially provided by a Western donor, through TrustAfrica, supported research and led to the articulation of a distinctly African agenda with input from across the continent. This new point of view attracted new constituencies, led to a multi-country people's campaign and is being advanced at the African Union, in consultation with TrustAfrica and its partners.

While the above examples, and others in this book, paint one view of the positive potential of donor funds on African agency, the reality with much philanthropy is that donors – local and global – too often play a very constraining role on local agency. Civil society organisations are replete with examples of how donor funding, no matter how well intentioned, has come with very particular strings attached. At times these strings are reflected in ideological or theoretical assumptions that may apply well in the global north but are not appropriate to the African context; at other times they are seen in demands that a particular type of strategy or programme focus be included in the work. Restrictions on flexibility of funding and preference for project-based rather than institutional support, coupled with the insecurity of short-term grant cycles, can severely constrain the agency of funded institutions to respond and programme in ways that are, in fact, demanded by very fluid and complex contexts, thus boring into the very heart of the notion of agency, and in fact limiting its scope.

These issues could equally apply to institutions such as TrustAfrica, which are both recipients and dispersers of funds. TrustAfrica, as an institution that receives funds from others, is itself vulnerable to some funding parameters from its own donors, which in turn places restrictions on its own agency to act freely. In turn, as a funder, it must also be mindful of the way in which its own funding processes, at times, have a constraining effect on the agency of its partners.

Alice Brown, looking quite intimately at the issue in Chapter 4, interrogates the notion of being both a funded and funding institution, and the complexities and challenges that arise. She asks: how much agency is really possible for an institution like TrustAfrica when it must negotiate funding parameters and timelines with its own donors? And what limitations do the negotiations then impose on how TrustAfrica engages with its own funded partners? One important implication is that it limits their ability to plan and strategise together over a multi-year period. Another is that it may prohibit follow-up activities that could expand shorter-term gains into longer-term victories. In some cases, these funding parameters have affected a partner's ability to retain its staff or jeopardise its ability to survive as an institution. A further consideration is that such funding restrictions can, at times, act as a barrier to more flexible and proactive work, with funded institutions playing what Abbas calls 'a firefighter role' rather than developing longer-term preventative strategies to tackle the issues. This speaks to the need for philanthropic institutions to invest in what Alicia Garza, a founder of the Black Lives Matter movement, calls 'long-term power building' (Friedman, 2016). In the absence of their own long-term sustainable resources, however, TrustAfrica and other like institutions find themselves navigating a tricky place: needing to advocate for and negotiate their own agency with their donors while simultaneously aiming to ensure that they devolve the power this agency brings with it.

The need for reliable, long-term funding emerges as a major issue in these chapters. As Abbas and Brown point out, promising movement-building work slowed considerably when donors ceased their funding, when the grant terms expired or when donors changed funding priorities. Several authors conclude that African philanthropic institutions need to have their own independent resources that they are able to use in a flexible way in response to real-time opportunities and needs they see on the ground. Control over the distribution of resources, irrespective of source, is thus a critical issue. In addition, cultivating local resources will reduce dependency on outside donors and, if combined with a ceding of power downwards, can enable a long-term focus on promoting agency and advancing social justice.

To be sure, African resources could easily replicate the power structures and modalities of the international aid system or international private philanthropy. What really matters is the way in which the funds are used: an approach that is rooted in locally dictated priorities, with decisions being informed by those most affected – an approach that in ideology is Africanist and in perspective is intersectional.

What does African agency look like?

Beyond the conceptual, the chapters in this volume add greatly to the understanding of what it means *in practice* to foster African agency. The diversity of approaches makes clear that there is no one way to do it. TrustAfrica's theory of change holds that civil society movements, if empowered, informed, networked and resourced, can effectively mobilise people to hold all levels of government – as well as other holders of power such as the private sector – to account. We see this play out in a myriad of ways in the book.

So what do these chapters tell us about TrustAfrica's work? The programmatic chapters collectively point us towards a set of 'ways of working'. While each factor is valuable in and of itself, their full impact emerges when they are presented together. These ways of working are by no means unique to TrustAfrica or to African philanthropy, but they are not the norm for philanthropy generally. Since the chapters themselves review these factors, this introduction will not go into detail but will rather illustrate some of the core elements and reflect on the issues and questions they raise.

Two uniting threads lie at the heart of TrustAfrica's work. These threads represent the very make-up of the institution and have carried through since inception, irrespective of changes in programmatic direction. The first is the idea of rootedness, which is linked to TrustAfrica's core identity as an African-led institution. The chapters in this book indeed reflect rootedness as one of the critical factors underlying its approach: it is based on the continent, in proximity to the issues and challenges, with staff committed to directly and indirectly supporting and enabling the work, not just resourcing it from afar. The chapters show that the impact of this rootedness plays out in several ways. For instance, Sipalla reflects on how having an African funder supporting international criminal justice work has not only opened doors and transferred a sense of legitimacy to its partners but also resulted in the creation of spaces for an African narrative to emerge. Brown reflects on how, through its physical presence in Liberia and Zimbabwe, TrustAfrica has been able to develop intimate relationships with multiple role-players and keep a finger on the pulse. She reflects, 'Its position on the frontlines allows it to be an integral part of the strategising and co-creation of solutions alongside civil society and other democratic actors'.

But is geographical location an adequate criterion of rootedness? We see many instances of local funding institutions advancing the idea that because they are locally based, they themselves (and not the partners doing the work or beneficiaries being affected by the issues) are experts and know best the nature of the development solutions that are required and need to be implemented. In such cases, rootedness can be used as a justification for centralising funding power to make decisions rather than reaching out to constituency voices to inform those funding decisions. The argument of rootedness thus needs always to be seen in context, and funders in general need to be mindful of geographic rootedness not being used as justification for holding on to power rather than disbursing it.

Hence it is important that rootedness be accompanied by something else. The second uniting thread is the idea of agency, which was earlier conveyed as the belief in and capacity of Africans to make their own choices about their future. How a philanthropic institution understands the agency of its partners is a key determinant of the ways in which it will operate, the nature of issues it engages and the types of strategies and tactics it will support. Supporting fully the idea of agency requires a relinquishing of power downwards to one's partners – this includes the power to determine priorities and solutions, the power to represent and speak on behalf of constituents, and the power to create knowledge and set agendas. Relinquishing power demands a mode of philanthropic operation that in every way is committed to enabling partners not only to be heard but also to exercise their influence.

What does it mean in practice, to devolve power? Despite concerns around limited funding cycles and uncertainty at the level of TrustAfrica's funding decisions, this relinquishing of power has, for instance, been reflected in the institution's approach of utilising convenings and knowledge building as the basis for developing collective agendas and funding priorities. This helps to ensure that resourcing decisions are based on the reality of local issues and priorities. Abbas views this as putting the work in context, and we need to note her caution that while the idea behind such methods is to broaden the range of voices informing its work, there is a very real danger that it still excludes those who are not networked in – potentially leaving non-traditional voices out of the discussions. At the same time, other authors observe that convenings and grounded research have served as key avenues for enabling different types of discussions and supporting more collaborative agenda setting than would otherwise be the case.

As Abbas points out, convenings alone are not enough to enable the priorities of those most affected to emerge: it also takes a concerted effort to reach out to marginalised communities in order to provide resources and enabling mechanisms for their voices to be heard. The ongoing challenge for philanthropy, even when moving beyond the networked, more visible organisations, is to constantly explore which are the non-institutionalised voices that need to be included. They are often not linked to the sector and lack information or networks. Indeed, often their plight has continued unabated because of their invisibility and lack of access. Sometimes, despite awareness of these voices, bureaucratic processes or difficulties in dealing with accessing disparate voices can result in the establishment of internal barriers within philanthropic institutions. When this happens, reaching these voices requires a different way of working, an opening to perspectives and voices that challenge our comfort zones.

The chapters show that a key endeavor of TrustAfrica has been to deliberately open up the civil society space. Sipalla notes the importance of TrustAfrica's reaching out to civil society beyond the 'urban, sophisticated African NGO so as to represent better the complex diversity of African societies'; Brown reflects on the deliberate inclusion of rural and marginalised constituencies; Mubaya discusses reaching out directly to farmers' member-based associations (rather than elite NGOs who seek to speak on their behalf); and Abbas looks at the inclusion of younger women as shifting the locus of power from the older generation. Several authors, however, caution that more can be done in this regard and that room could be made for even more diverse engagement – for instance, engaging with unaffiliated community organisers or small community based organisations, or exploring how to include the voices and priorities that are reflected in less institutionalised spaces of activism. It is also important to note that both Abbas and Brown suggest that gender has not been adequately incorporated into TrustAfrica's programmatic work, and call for a more integrated and substantive approach to be adopted in this regard.

Linked to efforts to expand and include multiple voices is the issue of movement building, i.e. developing a cadre of African organisations and individuals that can speak with a shared voice, develop collaborative agendas and advance collective policy positions. Several chapters highlight TrustAfrica's contributions to movement building. Brown sees this playing out in collaborative efforts to advance constitutional reforms in

Zimbabwe and in the work on natural resources concessions in Liberia. Ngirande reflects on how a movement-building approach has greatly helped to advance a more contextualised reflection of the IFF challenge in Africa, and Sipalla talks about this in relation to enabling the issue of victims' rights to take a much more central place in impunity work. Abbas argues that women's rights movements require quality resourcing, the kind that is possible only when funders apply a movement-building lens that is also African. Thus the funding itself needs to have a pan-African ideological base and an intersectional focus.

TrustAfrica considers resourcing as one of several core elements required for movement building and change. It seeks to adopt a holistic approach that complements grant funds with networking, institutional strengthening (both substantively and technically), leadership development, enabling knowledge generation and brokering between different and often unequal loci of power. Several of the chapters also reflect on how TrustAfrica's strategic approach to collaboration – which Murisa refers to as stemming from its aim to see itself as a 'landscape interpreter and an honest broker responsible for helping forge alliances' – has a significant effect on its work in many areas. It uses donor collaboratives to unite and expand the reach of previously disparate and sometimes duplicative funding mechanisms, and it uses partner collaboratives to broaden and deepen the impact of the collective programmatic work, amplify voices and enhance their power to influence policy and practice. This type of support is significant given the fact that such a strategic approach is relatively rare among funders. A recent report on global human rights funding, for example, shows that coalition and collaboration building received just 5% of grant dollars, and grassroots organising only 2% of grant dollars (Koob et al., 2016).

While several chapters make clear the value of TrustAfrica's collaborative approach, they also convey some important lessons for all of those who seek to undertake this kind of work. Brown, for instance, highlights the need to pay specific attention to the processes required to maintain healthy collaborations. Abbas suggests that developing collaborative mechanisms needs to be undertaken in a way that ensures that they are embedded and can continue beyond the role of the funder.

Another challenge for TrustAfrica and other philanthropies is to become better at working through an intersectional lens (see Abbas). As Murisa points out, while viewing our work in silos enables us to make sense of an issue, it simultaneously fragments it. We must therefore find ways to work more effectively together to advance social change across issues. Abbas also calls on us to support to an array of movement actors, recognising that limiting funding to institutionalised actors leads to fragmentation rather than movement building. This raises a larger question, also posed by Murisa: in a context where unorganised and distributed leadership movements are increasingly gaining and claiming space, what role is there for philanthropy? How best can philanthropy support them without trying to formalise them? What alternative avenues exist to facilitate spaces for these voices to be heard? Can the rules of engagement with broader civil society be revised to do so? Ultimately, the question needs to be posed: how open is philanthropy to confronting its own limitations in this regard?

A seat at the table

Gerry Salole, the founding chair of TrustAfrica's board,[9] has said that 'TrustAfrica allows Africans to take their rightful seat at the table among donors and others who influence development' (Barya and Richardson, 2012). TrustAfrica's aim has been to use this seat at the table – through its 'ways of working'– to advance two larger ends. First, to support the development of narratives, positions and priorities that reflect the lived realities of those suffering from injustice. Second, to support the use these narratives, positions and priorities to push for a more grounded understanding – at the seats of power – of the challenges being faced on the ground, and thus for more contextualised and locally defined solutions.

The chapters in this book show that TrustAfrica's support is enabling these ends in significant ways. Ngirande, for instance, reflects on how northern narratives on the issue of illicit financial flows had reinforced asymmetries of power. Because the existing narratives did not express or deal with the specificities of the African IFF problem, TrustAfrica and its partners undertook a movement building effort to reframe the debate on IFF. This, in turn, enabled a more holistic look at the structural weaknesses of the global ecosystem. Mubaya observes how TrustAfrica's approach highlighted the traditional dichotomy between policy advocates and small farmers, and created spaces, for the first time, for farmers' voices to be directly involved in the policy deci-

---

9   Salole was integral to TrustAfrica's establishment in his role as the Ford Foundation's representative in South Africa. He now heads the European Foundation Centre.

sions that affect their lives.

Advancing these ends is not easy in the larger scheme of how institutional philanthropy continues to play out, and the way in which an inequitably configured development system gives precedence to the experts and the educated elite. Progress requires implementing strategies that offer a distancing from the conventional wisdom, knowledge and expertise, and challenge existing frameworks and priorities. It also demands that a concerted effort be made to ensure that space is claimed for these narratives, positions and priorities to develop and build momentum – and that these be interjected into fora where they are able to exert influence over decision making.

For institutions such as TrustAfrica, this calls for taking on positions that may not be popular or widely accepted, and challenging dominant power relations that have long sought to define not just who sits at the decision making table, but what issues are up for discussion at that table. These locally informed narratives and positions seek to disrupt prevailing orthodoxies, and so institutions such as TrustAfrica consistently need to reflect on how to both challenge the systems and yet still retain influence within them. Or, seek to develop alternative systems. Through the examples in the book, TrustAfrica has seen success in using the leverage it has to diffuse power rather than centralise it. In this way it is enabling a shift of the balance of power relations from elites to people on the ground. It is indeed, African agency at work.

References

Barya, M.K. and W. Richardson (2012) *TrustAfrica: A Chronicle*, p. 16 Available at http://trustafrica.org/en/about-us/our-history. Accessed August 9, 2016.

Friedman, R. (2016) 'Moving Beyond a Movement Moment'. New York, International Human Rights Funders Group. Available at https://ihrfg. wordpress.com/2016/07/25/moving-beyond-a-movement-moment. Accessed on August 9, 2016.

Koob, A., S. Tansey and C. Dobson (2016) 'Advancing Human Rights: Update on Global Foundation Grantmaking'. Available at http://humanrights-funding.org/report-2016. Accessed on August 9, 2016.

Mahomed, H. and B. Moyo (2013) 'Whose Agenda? Power and Philanthropy in

Africa'. *Alliance*, 1 September. Available at http://www.alliancemagazine.org/feature/whose-agenda-power-and-philanthropy-in-africa. Accessed August 9, 2016.

Sowa, T. (2013) 'Interview: Theo Sowa'. *Alliance*, 1 September. Available at http://www.alliancemagazine.org/feature/interview-theo-sowa. Accessed August 9, 2016.

2

How To Make Societies Thrive:
The role of African Philanthropy

Bhekinkosi Moyo

Introduction

Historically, and in modern times, philanthropy, and in particular African philanthropy, has functioned as a glue that binds humanity, promoting solidarity and integration. It is the energy that animates collective action, unity, and self-reliance as well as the transformation of economic and social relations. It builds social cohesion through its emphasis on creating bonds and bridging difference. This has been consistently confirmed by communities and initiatives across Africa. For example, the liberation of many African countries was primarily based on philanthropic efforts, and testimony to this is found in the solidarity that was built from Algeria to South Africa, from Tanzania to Zimbabwe, and from Uganda to Mozambique, among others. In addition, communities bonded together and provided valuable support to liberation movements and the many other united fronts and self-reliance initiatives that were developed, for example by the Organisation of African Unity (OAU), in the 1960s through the 1990s. Today this imbedded interface between philanthropy and pan-Africanism continues in many of the initiatives and policies of the African Union (AU).[1]

This chapter discusses the state of African philanthropy today and

---

1 For a detailed discussion of the interface between pan-Africanism and African philanthropy, see Moyo and Ramsamy (2014).

the role it plays in promoting and projecting local agency. It also discusses its role in speaking truth to power, levelling the playing field and sustaining development. Philanthropy has been adopted by many African institutions. TrustAfrica was one of the first in a series of African institutions to formally develop a portfolio on African philanthropy.[2] The chapter therefore reflects on African philanthropy in its many forms including the institutionalised version. This is done in an era characterised by massive growth and interest in the field as well as by acute social, economic and political challenges which require the kind of solidarity mechanisms that are the hallmarks of African philanthropy.

Local agency and African philanthropy frame

In an article about TrustAfrica's efforts in influencing policies at a pan-African level, I equated local agency with philanthropy:

> As a foundation based in Africa, TrustAfrica is often in collision with political elites and others with vested interests. This is why we have adopted African agency or what we term African philanthropy. Africans should be at the centre of the response to their challenges and African philanthropy means resources – human, financial, social, intellectual – that can be tapped to address Africa's problems (Moyo, 2010a: 45).

Local agency is also defined in sociological terms as the capacity of individuals to act independently and make their own choices. To be sure, local agency is also determined by structural and systemic factors. It is therefore appropriate that any investigation of this nature should be interested in how philanthropy builds social cohesion and contributes to local capabilities and orientations as far as structures and systems are concerned. Many countries and societies in Africa in particular have local initiatives or practices that have historically provided the foundations for social transformation and social cohesion. These have been institutionalised and, often, modernised to frame the economic, social and political transformations needed to sustain societies. A case in point are local initiatives in Rwanda known as *ubudehe*, *Girinka Munyarwanda*, and *umuganda* (Ndahiro et al., 2015). Rwanda's celebrated success is firmly grounded in these practices in areas such as socio-economic transformation; good governance, justice, economic development and

---

2   Its 2007 Philanthropy Research and Outreach Strategy set in motion such initiatives as the formation of the African Philanthropy Network (APN), research initiatives and collaborations as we have them today.

social welfare. Elsewhere in East Africa, particularly in Kenya, the same practices are found and perhaps best captured in the concept of *harambee*. In Southern Africa, initiatives of this nature are underpinned by the concept of *ubuntu*.

Philanthropy and African identity are therefore inseparable. Although philanthropy transcends race and geography, it nevertheless remains one of the key features of African identity. Philanthropy permeates and to a large measure shapes many aspects of individuals, communities and institutions. Philanthropy, in the African context, is many things: a spirit, energy, power and any other form that makes humanity lovable. It connects life with death and rebirth.

The spirit of solidarity among African societies is what connects everyone and their aspirations. As I argued in 2011:

> Though not a common or even user-friendly concept in Africa, philanthropy as a phenomenon perhaps is best captured by the notions of 'solidarity and reciprocity' among Africans and some of the features that accompany relational building. As a result, therefore, culture and relational building are central attributes in defining what philanthropy in the African context looks like. Philanthropy is intrinsically embedded in the lifecycle of birth, life and death of many, if not all Africans. At any one given time, one is either a philanthropist or a recipient of one kind or another of benevolence. (Moyo, 2011: 1)

Seen in this light, philanthropy is an instrument of trust, accountability and mutual cooperation. It is those activities (mostly private) performed with a goal of promoting well-being. It can take many forms: individuals giving to nonprofit organisations; diaspora communities funding relief and development projects in their home towns; foundations and charities supporting community projects, social investments, and programme-related investments; corporations undertaking cause-related marketing campaigns as well as multi-million dollar disease treatment programs. It is members of religious organisations undertaking short- and long-term missions to help in orphanages; individuals using technology such as SMS to transfer funds to disaster victims and donating to overseas projects through the internet; and the use of entirely new financial tools, such as social stock exchanges, to promote well-being.

This is the prism through which any attempt to understand African philanthropy should be seen. It lays the basis for differentiation between

African philanthropy and typologies found elsewhere. It also makes clear that the establishment of institutions like TrustAfrica, the African Women Development Fund, and the Kenya Community Development Foundation among others, signalled the birth of a new defining era for African philanthropy. This era elevated the position of African philanthropy and begun unpacking the nuances and subaltern notions of what it means to be philanthropic in the African landscape and equally what it means to be African in the philanthropy landscape. With many of these institutions operating at national, regional, continental and global levels, there has been a resurgence of African pride and the belief in local agency.

Further, there has been recognition and reaffirmation of African identity and approaches. Nowhere do we see this more, than around the formation of African philanthropy support organisations such as the African Philanthropy Network, the Africa Philanthropy Forum, the East Africa Association of Grant Makers and many others that have emerged across the continent (Mahomed, 2014). There has been a huge upsurge of intellectual engagement with the subject; in the last fifteen or so years, the literature on African philanthropy has increased enormously.[3]

State of philanthropy in Africa and African philanthropy

> The philanthropic landscape in Africa is generally characterised by both horizontal and vertical dimensions. Because the term 'philanthropy' is not popular with the people in the continent, and neither is it useful in capturing what exists, the emerging body of literature on philanthropy in Africa prefers to define philanthropy as 'help' or 'giving'. Philanthropy refers to giving by the poor to other poor individuals of the community. More often this manifests itself in cultural and linguistic underpinnings – hence it normally takes on indigenous expressions such as co-operatives, rotation and savings clubs (normally called *stokvels*), communal collective efforts and burial societies. Philanthropy also takes forms such as private foundations, trusts, corporate foundations, family trusts, community chests and community foundations (Moyo, 2010b: 263).

Today, across the continent, and for the first time in history, African philanthropy, in particular international private foundations and new-

3 An African Giving Knowledge Database compiled by TrustAfrica shows that there are more than 800 writings on African philanthropy. The database can be accessed here http://www.trustafrica.org/en/philanthropy-database

found wealthy individuals, is beginning to take a central role in questions of development and sustainability and slowly informing policy processes at a national level. In 2009, for example, the government of Liberia established the Liberia Philanthropy Secretariat, a platform for linking national priorities with philanthropic resources primarily from foreign sources. In 2015, the AU launched the African Union Foundation to mobilise voluntary contributions in support of its Agenda 2063. Meanwhile, the Southern African Development Community (SADC) is in the process of developing a framework for the inclusion of philanthropic activities in support of its regional integration agenda. In Rwanda, the government is currently developing a strategy to engage philanthropy in implementing Vision 2020, while in South Africa, the National Treasury and Department of Science and Technology are doing the same.

Giving in Africa by Africans and international benefactors is on the increase. Recent research shows that US foundation funding for Africa increased from $288.8 million in 2002 to nearly $1.5 billion in 2014 (Foundation Center, 2015). The number of US foundations giving to Africa rose from 135 in 2002 to 248 in 2012. The bulk of the funding is for health, agriculture, water and sanitation, women's empowerment, youth employment and education.

Interestingly, more than 75% of this funding is administered by intermediary organisations headquartered outside Africa. In 2012, twelve of the top fifteen recipients of Africa-focused US foundation funding were headquartered outside of Africa. One of the arguments advanced for this is that local organisations do not have the capacity to absorb and manage large resources. This is not true. There has been a significant growth in institutionalised philanthropy in Africa. There are many African philanthropic institutions, most of which have been in existence for more than a decade. TrustAfrica for example, is celebrating ten years of existence in 2016, during which time it has managed more than $20 million and not once has it been found wanting. The same applies to many other such groups as the African Women's Development Fund, the Southern Africa Trust and the Nelson Mandela Children's Fund which were established precisely to 'change perceptions about Africa and to begin to imagine an Africa capable of deciding her own destiny' (Moyo, 2008: 40). Not only have they managed huge amounts of money, they have also been at the forefront of development initiatives and the setting of agendas. They have attempted to level the playing field between the traditional powerful Northern donors and beneficiaries in Africa, and have argued for the movement of resources closer to where the challenges are and advocated for Africans to be the drivers of change.

African giving is also on the increase, through corporations, family foundations, trusts, individual giving, voluntarism and community philanthropy. These include Aliko Dangote's Dangote Foundation (manufacturing), Strive Masiyiwa's Higher Life Foundation (telecommunications) and Tony Elumelu's foundation (investment banking). These so called high net worth individuals (HNWIs) are giving back to their communities and becoming forces to contend with. They see philanthropy as part of the African identity.[4] As the number of HNWIs grows, so too does the number of institutions, networks and organisations established by wealthy African individuals.

The number of Africa's HNWIs increased by 5.2% in 2014 to 0.15 million, while their wealth increased by 7.0% to $1.44 trillion. Globally, 14.65 million HNWIs have a total worth of $56.40 trillion. Africa has the fastest growing market of HNWIs in the world. It is further projected that Africans with assets more than $30 million will double by 2025, a growth of 59% over the next ten years compared to the global figure of 34% (Capgemini, 2016).

The number of philanthropists from the technology industry is growing globally; Facebook, Amazon and Uber, for instance, generate substantial wealth and giving.

There is also a moderate increase in faith-aligned philanthropies from the Middle East and Africa. Arab philanthropy has focused on either smaller familial networks or related issues, or has been tied to the spread of particular religious practices and beliefs.

The increased interest in the theory and practice on philanthropy has also led to the establishment of the Wits Business School Chair in African Philanthropy, a joint initiative with the Southern Africa Trust, and the first of its kind in Africa. The Chair will spearhead teaching and community engagement across the continent, produce internationally recognised research, foster innovation, and explore ways to strategise and support African-centric mechanisms of giving.

One can only conclude that there has never been a greater time for African philanthropy than today. The momentum and interest around it have grown – at times surprisingly so, given that not so long ago philanthropy was accorded no role in formal and intergovernmental processes. Not many governments considered philanthropy in their policy process-

---

4   See Mahomed et al. (2014).

es, and if they did, it was disparagingly or distrustfully. Today they have embraced philanthropy as an important resource for development. This is an opportunity to assert the role philanthropy plays in building social cohesion and local agency.

Social cohesion and individual empowerment

African people have always recognised the value of bonds that keep them together, which is why their struggles were mostly interlinked at community, national and global levels. This uncorrupted love and compassion led to many movements that were underpinned by features of African philanthropy such as unity, self-reliance, solidarity and reciprocity. All of this is framed by the philosophy of Ubuntu – 'one is because of the other'. It is this interdependence that makes philanthropy a very powerful paradigm for building social cohesion, developing local capabilities and shaping a world where no one should be left behind. At his trial in 1960, Nelson Mandela said: 'During my lifetime, I have dedicated myself to this struggle of the African people. I have fought against white domination, and I have fought against black domination. I have cherished the ideal of a democratic and free society in which all persons live together in harmony and with equal opportunities'.

Philanthropy has the power to build societies in amazing ways. Nowhere is this truer than in African societies. This is perhaps most poignantly demonstrated in post-genocide Rwanda, which revisited its traditions and sought to rebuild using its own systems and knowledge. 'To many observers, Rwanda is an example of how traditional culture can be a source of inspiration in finding solutions to modern day challenges' (Ndahiro et al., 2015: 312). The first instance of this is *Itorero,* a traditional leadership institution that taught values like nationalism, patriotism, hard work and honesty. This instilled in citizens the understanding and appreciation of their society and encouraged them to be ready to serve it. *Itorero* is open to all genders and the government has revived it and used it to train citizens about what it means to be Rwandan as well as equipping them with leadership skills. The second is the *Gacaca* ('justice amongst the grass') courts that were adopted to deal with cases of more than 120,000 individuals arrested for the genocide. The third is the *Agaciro* ('dignity') Development Fund, established to mobilise voluntary contributions to Rwanda's development. The fourth is *Girinka Munyarwanda* ('one cow per poor family'), a new initiative that was adapted from a traditional practice of solidarity where community members gave each other a cow as a pact of friendship and support in situations of misfortune or need. As in most African cultures, a cow is a sign of wealth and breaking of poverty. The programme was initiated specifically to deal with malnutrition and poverty. Today, Rwanda boasts that the programme has:

> Helped curb malnutrition, break down social barriers, improve agricultural output, support reconciliation efforts and greatly improved the welfare of hundreds of thousands of Rwandans (ibid.: 223).

The fifth is the popular *umuganda* – 'coming together in a common purpose'. Traditionally in Rwanda, community members would meet and jointly support one of their community members in constructing a house, for example, or farming or working on a community project. Nowadays, everyone comes together on the last Saturday of the month to participate in a five-hour community work programme. Sixth is the practice of *ubudehe* (mutual assistance), in which community members come together and identify the challenges confronting them and devise solutions by working together. Today, this practice is used by communities to identify the needy among them to benefit from programmes such as *Girinka*.

What is common among these initiatives is that they are all based on solidarity. They have also become the foundation for accountable governance. When parents build schools, they are the first to make sure children go to school, and that the principal manages the infrastructure properly. And when citizens contribute to the national budget by building health centres, offices and roads, they are the ones to demand accountability for the use of resources. These home-grown initiatives are not peculiar to Rwanda; they are found in other African countries too:

> Other forms of reciprocal giving include traditional systems of cooperation, mutuality and solidarity. These remain active today across African societies, 'primarily in rural areas as well in informal economic settings'. Among these are rotating savings and credit associations – popularly known as *stokvels* in South Africa but found everywhere across Africa. More often a group of people come together and pool their resources for a later redistribution. Beyond the savings and credit elements is the central value of mutual assistance. Burial societies are another form of African solidarity which initially played the role of cultural and societal compliance with rituals associated with death, es-

pecially for those who die far from their ancestral homes. Today these have incorporated a somewhat micro-insurance aspect to them; beyond the communal fundamentals of sending off the dead to the land of ancestors, burial societies now serve as financial backers for the bereaved. There are also other mechanisms for sharing labour-intensive ventures such as farming, house construction, harvesting or any other activity that might need mutual work-sharing. Known as *ilima* (coming together to help those without) among the Nguni-speaking people, this practice is widespread across Africa (Moyo, 2011: 7).

Civil society strengthening and movement building

Philanthropy has contributed to the growth and protection of civil society in addition to strengthening social cohesion. In Africa, governments have traditionally viewed philanthropy, particularly from international foundations, as forming part of the western agenda to influence regime change. This has been fuelled in part by the fact that foundations have supported civil society organisations on issues such as governance, human rights, poverty eradication, economic development and elections. Governments in Africa have not taken kindly to this, as it has tended to encourage citizens to hold them to account. The result has been the targeting of civil society, including philanthropy, by governments across the continent.[5]

Civil society's main role is to defend democratic values, so it is not unusual for it to be constrained by governments. As the American abolitionist, Frederick Douglass once said, 'Power concedes nothing without a demand. It never did and it never will'. And African governments in particular know this. Most of them came to power through the mobilisation of citizens demanding concessions. Historically, especially during the anti-colonial struggles, political and civil society lines were blurred. It is only after African liberation movements came into power that the lines became clear. Civil society has continued to play its watchdog function ever since. One-party states – and ironically even modern African democratically elected states – have all been wary of civil society. The more democratic the space has become, the more vibrant civil society has also become, but this has made the state more agitated. In turn civil society has been further emboldened and determined to hold the state, and increasingly the market, to account. This is a theatre in which

---

5   For more on civil society and the operating space, see Moyo (2010b).

philanthropy is an active participant and not just a spectator. While most international foundations were initially geared towards supporting new nationalist governments, there was a shift in the late 1970s towards human rights and social justice. This is at the time when most African governments were adopting the one-party state system and pushing into hiding all dissenting or critical voices.[6] The point here is that philanthropy cannot be viewed outside the confines of government-civil society relations.

Philanthropy has however managed to forge a narrative that it is flexible in its funding modalities, that it is a risk-taker and that it fosters innovation. This works well for civil society in all spaces, closed or open. For civil society to be able to perform its roles properly and effectively, it requires the kind of support that is provided in the main by philanthropy.

Government and philanthropy nexus

With the rise of these institutions and the growing interest in researching and writing on African philanthropy has come the attention of policy makers. This has created both opportunities and challenges for African philanthropy in the spaces normally reserved for the public and private sectors. Increasingly, philanthropy is forming part of the official development paradigm while continuing to strengthen communities and their formations. This is an exciting moment for philanthropy, but it is also one that could contribute towards the weakening of local agency. As noted elsewhere:

> There are concerns that this new era of philanthropy will lead to a collusion between philanthropy and governments in pursuing government agendas, which could be at the expense of civil society. No doubt, governments are clear about their need to engage philanthropy: they are engaging philanthropy in order to meet global and national targets; theirs is to align philanthropic interventions and resources with national priorities. Governments further recognise the value of risk taking, innovation and stakeholder engagements, which characterise philanthropy. These are not features to be found in any government, and yet increasingly citizens are pushing their governments hard on service delivery. It has become clear to some governments that they need philanthropy to provide these features (Moyo, 2016).

---

6   See Moyo (2005).

Clearly something significant is happening. Philanthropy is being stretched. This is due to its resources and what governments think they will get if they engage it. Most governments are facing the reality of declining ODA flows. This has forced many to think of alternative sources of support. Philanthropy has become one of the sources, and it is being actively courted by governments. The evidence is clear in many countries. Globally, in the consultations leading to the Fourth High Level Forum on Aid Effectiveness (held in Busan, South Korea in July 2012), African countries emphasised the need to shift from aid effectiveness to development effectiveness. The broad way in which the Busan Partnership for Effective Development Cooperation was crafted allowed for the accommodation of other forms of development resources, including philanthropy. This rethinking of development assistance has also been apparent in recent global processes. The International Conference on Financing for Development that took place in Addis Ababa in July 2015 produced an outcome document that was endorsed by the UN General Assembly and which spoke of the role that ought to be played by philanthropy and foundations:

> We welcome the rapid growth of philanthropic giving and the significant financial and non-financial contribution philanthropists have made towards achieving our common goals. We recognize philanthropic donors' flexibility and capacity for innovation and taking risks and their ability to leverage additional funds through multi-stakeholder partnerships. We encourage others to join those who already contribute. We welcome efforts to increase cooperation between philanthropic actors, Governments and other development stakeholders. We call for increased transparency and accountability in philanthropy. We encourage philanthropic donors to give due consideration to local circumstances and align with national policies and priorities. We also encourage philanthropic donors to consider managing their endowments through impact investment, which considers both profit and non-financial impacts in its investment criteria.[7]

Governments and intergovernmental agencies clearly see a potential role for philanthropy and they have already made up their minds on how they seek to benefit from it. Most governments are interested in the resources. If philanthropy provided about $30 million towards the implementation of MDGs, and if, as Brad Smith argues in his blog,

---

7   UN General Assembly Resolution A/RES/69/13 adopted on 27 July 2015.

foundations are projected to provide $364 billion of the $3.5 trillion required,[8] then philanthropy is a potential source of additional funding for governments.

This is an opportunity for philanthropy to reclaim local agency for civil society, reform restrictive laws and forge a partnership that builds on the contributions of each. For example, in designing government-philanthropy collaborations, philanthropy can demand that certain principles and values be in place in return for resources.

Wither African philanthropy?

In a context where African countries are turning increasingly inward for resources, the philanthropic sector is becoming more central, and African HNWIs are increasingly able to contribute to this development. What is critical is that philanthropic initiatives recognise the importance of an African understanding of community.

Philanthropy should therefore engage governments strategically and robustly while maintaining a critical independence. Principles of engagement ought to be collectively developed and agreed upon between governments and philanthropies. Philanthropy must insist on a seat at the policy making table in order to advance social justice and support democratic values. It also needs to continue supporting civil society and using its leverage with governments to push for appropriate reforms. There is no doubt that more governments will be developing philanthropy engagements. Indeed, they may have little choice given the declining support from bilateral and multilateral institutions. At the same time philanthropy must address some of the criticism that has been levelled against it, otherwise governments will disparage it when it demands reforms. When all is said and done, philanthropy is still a part of civil society, despite its current cordial relationship with governments. Civil society is organic and rooted in communities, while governments are transitory. Philanthropy can therefore help societies thrive and unlock their creative energies.

---

8   'Foundations will contibute $364 billion to SGDs'. Philanthropy News Digest, 24 May 2016.

References

Capgemini (2016) 'World Wealth Report 2016'. Paris, Capgemini.

Foundation Center (2015) 'Groundbreaking Research Reveals Changes in Funding for Africa'. Press release, 18 November. New York, Foundation Center.

Mahomed, H. (2014) 'Of Narratives, Networks and New Spaces-A Baseline Mapping of the African Infrastructure Sector'. Nairobi, Rockefeller Foundation.

Mahomed, H., L.A. Julien and S. Samuels (2014) 'Africa's Wealthy Give Back: A Perspective on philanthropic giving by wealthy Africans in sub-Saharan Africa-with a focus on Kenya, Nigeria and South Africa'. Zurich and Dakar, UBS and TrustAfrica.

Moyo, B. (2005) 'Setting the development agenda? U.S Foundations and the NPO sector in South Africa: A case study of Ford, Mott, Kellogg and Open Society foundations'. PhD thesis, University of the Witwatersrand.

Moyo, B. (2008) 'Can the new African foundations level the playing field?' *Alliance*, September.

Moyo, B. (2009), 'Establishing an Africa Grant Makers Network'. A Discussion document for the Inaugural Meeting, April 3-4, Accra.

Moyo, B. (2010a) 'Influencing policy at a pan-African level', *Alliance*, 15(4), pp. 45-46.

Moyo, B. (2010b) 'Philanthropy in Africa: Functions, Status, Challenges and Opportunities' in N. MacDonald and L.T. de Borms (eds), *Global Philanthropy*. London, MF Publishing.

Moyo, B. (2011) 'Transformative Innovations in African Philanthropy'. Paper commissioned by the Bellagio Initiative.

Moyo, B (2013) 'Innovations in African Philanthropy' in T.A. Aina and B. Moyo (eds) *Giving to Help, Helping to Give: The context and politics of African Philanthropy*. Dakar, Amalion Publishing.

Moyo, B. (2016) 'African philanthropy at the crossroads: changing the relationship between civil society and government', *Alliance*, forthcoming September.

Moyo, B. and K. Ramsamy (2014) 'African philanthropy, pan-Africanism and Africa's development', *Development Practice*, 24(5-6), pp. 656-671.

Ndahiro, A., J. Rwagatare and A. Nkusi (2015) *Rwanda: Rebuilding of a Nation*. Kampala, Fountain Publishers.

3

African Agency
in Contested Contexts:
A reflection on TrustAfrica's work in
international
criminal justice

Humphrey Sipalla

'The world supply of disinterested altruists and unconditional aid is very small indeed.'

Julius Nyerere[1]

Introduction

In 2016, TrustAfrica celebrates its first decade as an African foundation and leader in shaping African philanthropy on the continent. Its work is built on a commitment to African agency, the conviction that Africans are the rightful drivers of efforts aimed at the transformation of their condition. This notion of agency is complicated, however, in the case of TrustAfrica's International Criminal Justice (ICJ) Fund. In this field, which seeks international justice for victims of crimes such as atrocity,

---

1   Nyerere (1970).

opinions are sharply divided over what it means for Africans to support Africa. This chapter discusses TrustAfrica's work in this contested setting, where a truly African theory and practice of philanthropy is emerging.

The ICJ Fund is a multi-donor fund whose vision is an Africa without impunity for perpetrators of international crimes.[2] The fund seeks to strengthen the capacity of local African civil society organisations (CSOs) to combat impunity through supporting social movements, elevating the voices of victims, and concerted advocacy for domestic, regional and international accountability mechanisms. The fund works to generate improved knowledge and understanding of international criminal justice and related issues. Its theory of change is that a well-informed citizenry and concerted civil society advocacy will provide the impetus for African leaders to address the scourge of impunity.

The fund was created in 2012 as a response to the growing backlash in Africa against the International Criminal Court (ICC), depicting the ICC as a pro-Western, imperialist organisation that disproportionately targeted Africans. Such depictions had overshadowed the need to secure justice on the continent. Although originally established to bolster African support for the ICC, the fund's understanding of what it means to be an African grant maker supporting African agency in a polarised setting has evolved, become more nuanced. This chapter sets out to discuss this evolution.

A history of the notion of African agency

The colonial enterprise, which any reflection on Africa's present and future can only ill-advisedly ignore, was built around denigrating the colonial subject (Fanon, 1963). Early assertions of African agency like the Negritude movement, which arose in the 1930s, relied on artistic expressions of cultural pride to reject the denigration of Africans and their descendants. It was not long, however, before Africans began to point

---

2   In our present context, these are genocide, war crimes, and crimes against humanity. The atrocities such crimes entail are considered so grievous as to 'deeply shock the conscience of humanity' and thus are of 'concern to the international community as a whole' especially as they 'must not go unpunished' with a view to 'end impunity and [thus] contribute to their prevention'. See Preamble of the Rome Statute of the International Criminal Court. However, international crimes may, in a larger context, also refer to crimes that threaten international peace and security, such as the crime of aggression, or crimes that necessarily occur beyond the normal jurisdiction of one state, such as piracy.

to the future of African agency, where spoken affirmations of cultural self-worth alone would not suffice. For instance, Wole Soyinka sharply criticised Negritude thus: 'A tiger does not proclaim his tigritude, he pounces.'

In the 1950s, as Africans fought for political independence, so urgent and necessary a task was it to assert African agency that Kwame Nkrumah, in his 'Motion of Destiny' speech in 1953, argued for the right of Africans to make their own mistakes as all peoples do.

The establishment of the Organisation of African Unity (OAU) embodied this conviction that official African action would be directed by Africans. However, while the elimination of oppression and discrimination had been a 'major factor in the African drive to self-determination and independence, the initial post independence [human rights] record of African states was generally unsatisfactory' (Jallow, 2012). It was sadly not unusual for African states to focus on the evils of apartheid while ignoring the 'massive and systemic violations, sometimes of a genocidal scale', amongst OAU members.

With Africans exercising their right to make mistakes, people began to demand more from African agency than rebuttals of cultural inferiority and recitals of lofty dreams.

African agency as improving the lot of Africans

In the academy, Wole Soyinka was insisting that the tiger ought pounce more than roar. Among statesmen, Julius Nyerere was already in 1970 showing dissatisfaction at the then prevailing trend of speaking in dreamy solidarity:

> [I]t is no longer enough [...] to meet and complain to each other and to the world. [...] Simply to meet and repeat our goals and intentions is, therefore, meaningless. Worse, it would imply that we have doubts about ourselves, and our ability to continue along the path that we have chosen for ourselves.[3]

Léopold Sédar Senghor, speaking in 1979, exemplified the decidedly introspective turn in assertions of African agency: 'Unfortunately, independent Africa hardly teaches a thing or two on human rights. Let us admit our weakness. It is the best method of getting over it.'[4] From Nkrumah fighting for a right to make mistakes, it was now time to own

---

3   Nyerere (1970).

4   At the opening the first meeting of the Drafting Committee for the African Charter on Human and Peoples' Rights in Dakar (Jallow, 2012: 62).

up to those failures.

On the official level, the most momentous change was that of replacing the OAU with the African Union (AU) in 2001. This was far from a simple name change. The OAU had been focused on eliminating colonialism and apartheid, and it considered state sovereignty as an absolute. The AU, on the other hand, has been described as the product of a paradigm shift in African official thinking, from OAU's policy of non-interference to a policy of non-indifference. Institutionally, the AU envisioned the creation of a court of justice to hold African states to account for international obligations, and a parliament that would progressively take over legislative powers from the Assembly of Heads of State and Government. It envisioned a wider set of institutions to engage in policymaking, such as the AU Peace and Security Council. Significantly, it absorbed the institutional vision of the 1991 African Economic Community Treaty that aimed to revamp and integrate African economies. On the accountability front, fresh with the memory – and guilt – of the 1994 genocide in Rwanda, the AU appropriated the bold legal right of the Union to intervene in any member state to stop the commission of international crimes – genocide, war crimes or crimes against humanity – under Article 4(h) of the Constitutive Act.[5]

Beyond responsibility: African agency as accountability

In the few years of the twenty-first century, the question of the true nature of African agency has become nuanced, especially in the context of Senghorian candour about Africa's human rights failings. Clearly, African agency must start with Africans being in charge of the decisions that affect their lives, even if this may involve making mistakes. But does African agency include African accountability for any such mistakes? How does Africa assert pride in itself while being frank about its failings? Are the old ideas of absolute African state sovereignty and non-interference valid? Who among the Africans, between perpetrator and victim, governor and the governed, holds rights to speak on our behalf? How do well-meaning Africans confront state failure while working with the authorities? What is an authentic African response to impunity for egregious human rights violations? And, are those who denigrate Africans necessarily non-African? These questions

5   To be sure, in the past African states had, haphazardly and in national self-interest, intervened in other countries, even militarily, as Tanzania did in 1979 to oust Idi Amin and ECOMOG, led by Nigeria, did in Liberia and Sierra Leone. But these were mostly exceptions to OAU policy.

are central to any conception of African philanthropy.

African agency without African money?

The implicit North-South divide that characterised assertions of African agency from the earliest times seems to have a tenacious hold, especially as concerns the question of sources of finance. Benjamin Mkapa, speaking on peace-building and transitional justice in Africa in 2014, offers this reflection:

> African mediators constitute an essential part of the post Cold War pattern of local and regional actors seeking solutions to local and regional problems. [...] Although there has been significant movement in reducing the competition between African and international actors over management, organisation, and ownership of mediation, a lot more needs to be done to establish functional and fruitful collaborative governance in mediation. *Resource imbalances between African and international mediators are not going to go away soon.* And when some international actors deride the capacity of African mediators, hostilities between local and international mediators deepen. On the other hand, some African actors have the tendency to diminish the significance of international contributions particularly in the event of successful mediation outcomes (Mkapa, 2016 [emphasis added]).

Issa Shivji (2005) captured the evolution of global political economy and the challenges to African agency that it poses to African philanthropy. Shivji distinguishes between civil society actors and non-governmental organisations,[6] locating the African NGO at the 'crossroads of the defeat of the national project and rehabilitation of the imperial project',[7] which recalls the century of evolving debate on African agency recounted above.

---

6   Civil society is traditionally defined as the space between the individual in private life and the state. Philanthropy necessarily acts within this space, which encompasses a wide variety of actors, from small community associations to trade unions and national and international networks. However, in twenty-first century Africa, this space, Shivji points out, has become dominated by the donor-funded NGO. He characterises NGO self-perception as a 'non-governmental, non-political, non-partisan, non-ideological, non-academic, non-theoretical, not-for-profit association of well-intentioned individuals dedicated to changing the world to make it a better place for the poor, the marginalised and the downcast'.

7   See Shivji (2005) 'By Way of a Preface'.

Shivji's is admittedly a 'ruthless self critique'.[8] He laments the 'false bi-polarity or dichotomy between the state and civil society' in Africa. In the context of resource imbalances, Shivji wonders whether the do-nor-funded African NGO is conscious of the ideological undercurrents of social change activism or is an unwitting player in what he calls a new-age civilising mission.[9]

Concurrent to the North-South divide is the divide within African societies. The African NGO form dominates the civil society space. Yet, does this NGO form adequately express the concerns of the lowly African, who in the context of international criminal justice, is the victim of atrocity crimes? To be sure, in the early years of African agency, it was assumed that any African spoke for all Africans. In twenty-first century Africa, this is not always the case. Are the views of local movements such as neighbourhood associations, victims' groups or rural communities influential in setting agendas and forming policy? Is a bottom-up model possible if these local voices remain dependent on resources outside their communities?

A prominent official African challenge to accountability advocacy is the peace versus justice debate that argues that conflict-weary communities prioritise an end to conflict. Seeing international criminal justice as a component of justice and reconciliation efforts, the African NGO is challenged to 'pursue holistic approaches that ensure justice for victims of gross human rights violations' (TrustAfrica and MacArthur Foundation, 2011). To achieve this, the civil society space ought allow for other CSO actors beyond the urban, sophisticated African NGO, so as to represent better the complex diversity of African societies.

An overview of the ICJ Fund

At the turn of the century, African NGOs and intelligentsia had viewed the AU's policy shift to non-indifference, the establishment of the Afri-

---

8   Shivji centres his critique of the African NGO form around five points he calls 'silences': a self-definition that emphasises a non-state bi-polarity; prioritising activism before understanding the phenomena to be changed; accepting the present state as permanent; the depoliticisation of civil society action that disregards the complexity of social interests and social justice; and ambiguous change theory that separates African activism from African intellectualism.

9   In this battle for the African soul, Shivji's arguments seem echoed by Gathii (2011), who posits that, insofar as neo-liberal trade agreements are concerned, developing countries are no longer hapless victims of Western imposition, but eager and willing adopters.

can Court on Human and Peoples' Rights and the strong official African support for the ICC, as heralding a new dawn for respect for human rights and fighting impunity. Yet, between 2005 and 2010, the sharp reversal in official support for existing accountability mechanisms raised concern among Africa's human rights community.

In November 2011, a meeting was organised by TrustAfrica, the Centre for Citizen Participation in the African Union (CCPAU) and the MacArthur Foundation in Nairobi to reflect on this troubling trend. The 58 participants were drawn from African NGOs, think tanks, donor institutions and African intellectuals, and sought to define an effective advocacy response to the ICC backlash. Participating donor institutions agreed to explore the possibility of joint funding in order to leverage the impact of individual donors and reach a more diverse group of African CSOs working on international criminal justice. The resulting fund, the TrustAfrica International Criminal Justice Fund, became operational in 2012.

The fund sets out its strategy thus: to strengthen the capacity of human rights organisations to contribute to transitional justice policymaking at the national level; and to develop informed and concerted advocacy strategies to promote international criminal justice at the regional and international levels. This strategic choice envisioned the following outcomes: 'Increased knowledge and understanding of the African international criminal justice landscape; Improved advocacy capacity of civil society organisations; Discernible improvements in responses to atrocity crimes' (TrustAfrica, 2015: 13).

The fund engages in three classes of activities: technical assistance (commissioned research mapping out the ICJ landscape in Africa, nationally, regionally and internationally); peer learning convenings; and grants, which constitute the principal activity of the fund.

A fiery baptism in 2012

The fund's earliest strategy statement had an almost exclusively ICC focus. In 2012, the fund planned to make two main clusters of grants: for national campaigns on ratification, domestication and monitoring implementation of the Rome Statute; and for regional and international campaigns on developing cooperation policies with the AU organs, or urging the ICC Prosecutor and the UN Security Council to consider cases from elsewhere in the world. The fund aimed to support the following activities: advocacy training and skills building; Rome Statute ratification and domestication campaigns and media outreach; dialogues and partnerships between states and advocacy organisations; and networking and coalition building among advocacy organisations. In addition, the fund planned rigid funding caps for its two classes of grants: $50,000 for national projects and $100,000 for regional or international projects.

A project was supported for civil society advocacy during the July 2012 AU Summit in Malawi. The Summit did not materialise, because Malawi refused to invite Sudanese President Omar al-Bashir. It was moved at the last minute to Addis Ababa, resulting in tensions that made for a particularly hostile ICC advocacy environment; the project was thus changed to support domestic public interest litigation, research and a conference on accountability for atrocity crimes in South Africa.

This very first project became emblematic of the politically charged and highly fluid nature of international criminal justice advocacy. If ever the fund had expected to apply its initial strategy rigidly, the circumstances of this project made it evident that a more nuanced approach was necessary.

During the course of 2012, TrustAfrica took two important steps. First, it recruited dedicated staff for the ICJ Fund. Second, it commissioned local experts to conduct eleven scoping studies on the international criminal justice landscape in ten specific countries and the AU. These studies became the foundation of the fund's model of knowledge management, which favours local expertise and promotes proximity to local concerns. The fund did not issue its second grant until October 2013.

Scoping studies as knowledge from the periphery

The fund spent the period between late 2012 and mid-2013 conducting scoping studies in Kenya, Uganda, the Democratic Republic of Congo, Egypt, Nigeria, Ivory Coast, Senegal, Guinea, Mali, Uganda, Sudan and the AU. The studies depicted each country's (and the AU's) specific political and legal issues and made recommendations of potential areas of action and local partners. Some, such as the Egypt report, presciently foresaw a significant reversal of democratic gains following the 2011 Arab Spring.

The studies affirmed the value of local expertise. Some also identified local actors who may not have been well known to international donors, but who stood to be potential partners and grantees.

In 2015 and 2016, the fund commissioned additional studies, on the implications of the unexpected arrest of former Lord's Resistance Army commander Dominic Ongwen, the situation in Uganda, and the ICJ landscape in Cameroon and the Central African Republic.

Principles of a nuanced and evolving grants policy

Attention to local context

In contrast to the initial grants policy described earlier, the fund's current practice seems more contextually appropriate. In Nigeria, for instance, given the high probability of pursuing Rome Statute domestication[10] and the need for documentation of victims as identified in the scoping study, the fund supported the work of the Nigerian Coalition for the ICC (NCICC). In Uganda, the political climate allowed for a first-ever attempt to bring together war victims across several decades to a national platform. On the other hand, as opposed to the situation before 2011, with the election of two Kenyan indictees to the highest political offices, Kenya replaced Sudan as the source and locus of a sustained state-driven campaign to delegitimise the ICC. Funding to Uganda and Kenya projects has reflected this, and has included a mix of regional and international advocacy by Kenyan and other African NGOs, engaging the national discourse on domestic prosecution (the proposed International Crimes Division of the High Court of Kenya), pro-active media engagement to balance the public narrative, and raising the profile of the victims who consistently get lost in the highly politicised Kenyan environment.

Victim centredness

The fund's early documentation did not mention 'victim' even once, but it has since placed significant focus on victim-centred projects; indeed, the first two grants approved in 2013 were entirely victim-centred. All grants currently incorporate an element of victim promotion, such as coalition building that involves victims' groups, litigation or advocacy that raises aspects of victims concerns, and research or documentation

---

10   'Domestication' is the process by which states convert international treaties they have ratified into locally enforceable laws. This is traditionally seen as a requirement in countries that follow the English common law tradition which sees international law as separate from national law. Such legal systems are thus termed 'dualist'. Most other countries however follow a 'monist' system by which the ratification of a treaty automatically makes it enforceable by local courts. Nigeria, being of dualist Common Law tradition, applies the 'domestication' requirement.

work that similarly incorporates victim-centred approaches. It is safe to say the fund has made victim-centred project design central to its work. Fund documentation from 2016 makes the focus on victims a necessary theme rather than a simple sub-category.

Flexible funding limits

Current practice now regards the $50,000 and $100,000 as guidelines rather than rigid limits. The lower category of grants is issued to new grantee partners to allow the fund to either acquire first-hand experience of their organisational capacities or grow such capacities where pre-funding assessments have noted weaknesses. First-time partners may receive more than $50,000 on the strength of excellent reviews.[11] At present, grants range from $30,755 to $150,000. The highest grant amounts so far approved for first-time partners are $110,000, $103,000 and $100,000.

While it would have been easier to retain rigid funding caps, the fund attempts to instead make its evaluation on a case-by-case basis, prioritising the project needs and organisational capacity over fixed internal limits. This has allowed for more effective projects, such as AYINET's 2014 National War Victims Conference, which was the first time that local victims' associations had been afforded a platform to share among themselves and directly voice their aspirations to state officials.

Civil society movement building

Another benefit of this move away from rigid funding caps is seen in the fund's focus on civil society movement building (including a media constituency), with sometimes small but bold grants.[12] Such a focus is central to the idea of TrustAfrica supporting African agency. In fact, the proportion of total investment devoted to movement building was 42% between 2012 and 2015, and this could only have been achieved with flexible funding. The fund applies a progressive growth principle that facilitates its commitment to going off the beaten path to identify under-

---

11   Factors include recommendations by other donors who have worked with the organisation in question, previous handling of grants of a similar value, and evidence of sound financial and project management systems.

12   Grants to *Coalition malienne des défenseurs des droits humains* (COMADDH), Southern Africa Litigation Centre (SALC), Kenya Chapter of the International Commission of Jurists (ICJ-K), *Association des femmes africaines pour le recherche et le développement* (AFARD), Nigerian Coalition for the ICC (NCICC), African Youth Initiative Network (AYINET) and Journalists for Justice (JFJ) are notable examples.

served constituencies and grow their capacities with incremental multi-year grants. The fund thus serves as a facilitator, providing support and expertise in grant application and execution to small organisations and allowing them time and opportunities to grow.

Movement building is approached from national and regional levels. In Mali, for instance, grants have included support to strengthen a national network of human rights advocates, facilitating the national secretariat's efforts to work with rural affiliates. By illustration, women's groups from across the country engaged in research data collection that valorised their local knowledge but also strengthened their connections to the national network. In Uganda, support for follow-up activities from the war victims conference focused on cementing the incipient victims' movement that had for decades been split into regional groupings.

Peer learning

The fund applies a peer learning approach to the meetings and conferences it supports. For instance, when supporting the 2014 AYINET conference, the fund ensured that grantee partners from other African countries attended, to see what best practices could be learnt from their Ugandan fellows. Uganda has one of the longest running conflicts in Africa, and was the first country in the world to set up a truth commission, in 1974, as well as the first to refer cases to the ICC.

This event made deep impressions on some of the fund's grantee partners from Kenya, Ivory Coast and Mali; the relative youth of their conflicts means victims' associations remain deeply divided along the same sectarian lines that fuelled the conflicts in the first place.

Similarly, the Southern Africa Litigation Centre (SALC) incorporated fund partners in its workshop to reflect on the status of international criminal justice at the continental level and in national litigation. ICJ Kenya and the Council for the Development of Social Science Research in Africa (CODESRIA) have been supported to nurture other African NGOs by involving them in their advocacy missions at the AU and ICC Assembly of State Parties. Other peer learning activities include the annual international criminal justice convening, which provides a platform for partners to share experiences. These activities enable the fund to build the capacity of its partners while itself learning from the participants.

The basket fund principle

As at end of 2015, the fund had seven primary donors: the John D. and Catherine T. MacArthur Foundation, the Oak Foundation, the Open Society Human Rights Initiative, the Open Society Foundation, Humanity United, the Sigrid Rausing Trust and an anonymous donor. These seven, together with TrustAfrica, pool their resources in a basket fund. In the case of the ICJ Fund, TrustAfrica is both grantee and equal partner. It does not simply serve as an outsourced administrator for the primary donors but as an active driver of policy and practice. A Steering Committee composed of these eight sets policy and manages the work of the fund.

Advantages of the basket fund approach

According to members of the Steering Committee, this resource pooling helps eliminate duplication when donors operate separately and allows for better trends analysis to avoid over-concentration in thematic or geographical areas. It also enhances the impact of overall interventions, and serves to build consensus on the best possible approaches to challenging impunity for atrocity crimes. This also helps prepare the fund for the long-term nature of international criminal justice advocacy.

The diversity of donors enables the rich range of innovative approaches the fund is currently engaged in. While one donor may emphasise documentation, and another prioritise movement building, a third may focus on pro-ICC advocacy. Interventions range from a focus on international structures of criminal accountability, through promotion of continental and national accountability structures, to support for victim concerns and overall transitional justice actions (documentation, truth telling, reconciliation, reparations).

By working in concert within the fund, grant makers are challenged to consider supporting activities that would otherwise have fallen outside their purview. The AYINET conference, for instance, was supported by the fund despite it having been earlier rejected by one of the fund's basket donors.

With small staff and large portfolios, grant makers are not always able to fund as many interventions as they would like. The diversity of local contexts, grant makers' location far from said contexts and administrative bottlenecks mean their involvement in Africa has often been far from optimal. The fund allows them to expand their reach and support the type or depth of projects they may not have supported if working individually.

Challenges of operating as a basket fund

No worthy endeavour is without its challenges. For the basket fund, these proceed from two key factors: first, the presence of several primary donors means that several distinct approaches have to be harmonised; second, the power dynamics within the Steering Committee require constant diplomacy from all concerned, and especially TrustAfrica, as both a grantee of and equal partner to its primary donors.

A key task for TrustAfrica in the basket fund is one of harmonising these diverse interests. But it also requires each donor to seek the common interest. This is not always easy. For instance, peer learning among grantee partners, which promotes the fund's efficacy, also requires increased expenditure on meetings, something that is not always popular among donors. Also, finding and supporting new CSO actors is time- and capital-intensive.

The Steering Committee faces the challenge of continuous introspection of its role. Should it make overall policy or participate in specific decision making? Should a donor be allowed to veto an approach or place upon a meeting's agenda, a review of an intervention that does not fit its preferred approach? Ought a donor be allowed to know what proportion of their investment in the basket goes into a particular project? And how does a donor conduct oversight of its own grant making in such a basket fund effort?

TrustAfrica mitigates these challenges by maintaining stringent internal administrative controls, as it is a trustee of its primary donors' funds. TrustAfrica must also maintain a constant diplomatic poise, using carefully crafted meetings to hear and respond to any queries from its donor partners. This is not always easy: a simple conference call from Dakar can be difficult to organise, given poor connectivity and varied time zones. Fund staff must also synthesise documentation from all the fund's activities to be discussed at SC meetings.

Certain attributes of the ICJ Fund

Close relationships with partners

The fund's secretariat has developed working methods which funded partners have described as respectful, conducive to capacity-building and sensitive to local needs. It is this strength that affords the fund its ability to respond effectively to the dynamic and complex circumstances it works in. Staff of the fund take time to get to know their prospective partners, to understand their weaknesses, and in some cases to help them draft their applications.

Such an approach is fraught with pitfalls. A grant maker must, by definition, sit in judgement over its partners, not only at the application stage, but throughout the grant period. The fund needs to support weak prospective partners without compromising objectivity. This applies both substantively and administratively. Expanding grant making to underserved communities also adds critical administrative questions such as monitoring project costs, which can only poorly be assessed from outside their context.

Seeking out underserved communities and NGOs

The African landscape of human rights advocacy and, by extension, international criminal justice, is largely dominated by the urban NGO, staffed by well-educated, soft-skilled[13] Africans in mostly English-speaking Africa. The donor community acting in African human rights advocacy is dominated by players from the Anglo-Saxon world. By contrast, French, Portuguese and Arabic non-African donors are scarce. And the typical civil society actor, particularly in French-speaking Africa, is a national association of many grassroots associations, with a limited national secretariat. Their constituency and staffing is likely to lack the soft skills needed to penetrate the English-speaking philanthropy world.

The fund has focused on reversing this trend by seeking out small, poorly resourced NGOs with a strong grassroots constituency, and deploying larger ones to support capacity building among them. The fund has taken affirmative action to facilitate the incorporation of poorly resourced NGOs that do not fit the dominant characteristic of the urban sophisticated English-speaking NGO.

The fund shuns the usual 'call for proposals' model, which tends to favour the well-resourced, experienced NGO, not least because they would be connected by internet to the virtual networks where such calls are distributed. Instead, the fund invites potential organisations to conversations aimed at synergising common aims.

Thanks to this approach, the fund's partners include a number of non-urban associations from English-speaking Africa and even larger number of associations from French-speaking Africa that had hitherto

13   By 'soft skills', we mean the intangible cultural understandings, demonstrated in language, etiquette and general diplomatic manner that would endear one, at a personal level, to interlocutors. Such skills better dispose a person to multicultural exchanges, which are necessary for inter-personal relations with Western donors.

been unable to attract significant funding. Coupled with a multi-year funding approach, a number of initially weak associations have grown in capacity and skills; they implement ever larger projects, and can apply their new skills to approach other donors with more stringent entry requirements. The fund thus becomes both benefactor and facilitator.

African identity versus African money

In international criminal justice advocacy, where the prevailing official narrative is that international mechanisms seeking accountability for mass atrocities are neo-imperialist, the fund's African identity bears great import. A number of the fund's partners have indicated that simply being funded by an African donor makes advocacy before state authorities more feasible. In their words, it 'opens doors' that would otherwise be locked. But as we have seen, TrustAfrica is itself funded by Western donors. This then begs the question of whether African identity necessarily requires African money.

In its 'Africanness', the fund presents one viable response to the conundrum of African philanthropy, given the very limited supply of disinterested altruists that Nyerere described, and the even more limited share of African philanthropists supporting human rights work, disinterested or otherwise. While Africa must progressively build its own 'bank' of indigenous philanthropy to build African civil society, Nyerere's call can also be seen as a challenge of substance. African money can be used to the detriment of Africa. Further, donor finance, regardless of its source, may cement top-down approaches, where the local and the periphery lose even the little say over their lives that they already have. If African philanthropy can apply models that empower the African periphery while utilising Western sources of finance, then the greater the benefit for Africans.

One answer may lie, if the fund's practice is anything to go by, in the model that is applied by African states themselves. The true disinterested altruist is one who listens to and responds to the needs of the subaltern, rather than dictating terms because they hold the purse strings. African states themselves seek funding from beyond the continent. What makes their action Afrocentric is not therefore the source of funding but where the decision-making agency lies. The African state can claim a mandate to govern, but good governance demands, of the state, the philanthropist and the NGO, not simply to speak for the periphery, but to allow themselves to be changed by the priorities of these peripheral communities.

Bridging NGO-academy, NGO-state dichotomies

The fund has made efforts to ensure that an intellectual understanding of the phenomena it seeks to act in favour of is at the core of and precedes its action. We have explored some examples above. In addition, the fund has sponsored projects seeking to bring African activism together, not only with the intelligentsia, but also with the state. It has been helpful that international criminal justice is itself ripe for such encounters. There is significant public discussion of the complexities of accountability for atrocities in Africa across the intelligentsia, NGOs and states. In fact, a good number of the thought leaders in this regard can be seen as intellectuals who work with state (nationally or internationally) and/or civil society. CODESRIA, for example, is arguably the premier African centre for social sciences scholarship, and is an inter-governmental organisation as well. CODESRIA's continental conference on International Criminal Justice, Reconciliation and Peace in Africa: the ICC and Beyond, held on 10-12 July 2014 in Dakar, brought together intellectuals, activists and state authorities to debate the complexities of international criminal justice in Africa.

Opportunities for the future

Official hostility to ICJ in Africa is far from universal

African diversity is also evident at the official level. African countries such as Botswana, Tanzania, Zambia and Malawi have shown a willingness to uphold their Rome Statute obligations. Further, African countries also practice a different foreign policy as individual countries as opposed to when acting within the AU. The Seychelles, Tunisia, Cape Verde and Côte d'Ivoire ratified the Rome Statute after 2010.[14] Botswana ratified the amendment to Rome Statute Article 8 and the amendment on the crime of aggression in 2013.[15] Gabon, Senegal and Uganda have ratified the Agreement of ICC Privileges and Immunities in 2010, 2009 and 2014 respectively.[16] These sovereign actions have occurred despite

---

14   https://asp.icc-cpi.int/en_menus/asp/states%20parties/african%20states/Pages/african%20states.aspx; https://www.icc-cpi.int/cdi Accessed 24 July 2016.

15   https://treaties.un.org/Pages/ViewDetails.aspx?src=TREATY&mtdsg_no=XVIII-10-a&chapter=18&lang=en Accessed 1 July 2015.

16   https://treaties.un.org/Pages/ViewDetails.aspx?src=TREATY&mtdsg_no=XVIII-13&chapter=18&lang=en Accessed 1 July 2015.

repeated AU decisions resolving non-cooperation with the ICC. Attention to this diversity can help cultivate a healthier democratic space in continental affairs where divergent views are not necessarily seen as disloyalty to Africa. The fund has for instance engaged the goodwill of the Senegalese state – given the election of Senegalese Justice Minister Sidiki Kaba to the ICC-ASP Presidency, and the trial of Hissène Habré – towards greater African state support for accountability efforts.

Arguing against de-funding pro-ICC engagement

After a decade of persistent African official hostility to accountability for international crimes, and the collapse of the dockets relating to Sudan and Kenya in 2015 and 2016, there is currently little appetite in the donor and NGO communities for pro-ICC engagement, unlike in 2011. Rather than divest from ICC advocacy, the fund may well consider sustaining its initial limited pro-ICC support long enough for it to bear fruit, at least in those countries where incumbent high-ranking officials are not indictees, which essentially means the vast majority of African cases before the ICC. As Uganda's experience demonstrates, by the close of 2013 a lack of movement in the LRA indictments had led the ICC Office of the Prosecutor to begin withdrawing active work in Uganda. This all turned around with the unexpected arrest of Dominic Ongwen, which reinvigorated interest in the ICC in Uganda, as well as rekindling concern for all the other victims of conflicts not covered by ICC action in Uganda.

Reversing the sidelining of the African human rights system

Accountability for mass atrocities can be seen to involve the two interrelated concerns of victim protection and redress, traditionally the province of human rights law,[17] and individual criminal responsibility. The history of recent international law shows that victims are more likely to be redressed in the flexible arms of international human rights law than the stringent walls of international criminal law.[18]

---

17   'The international protection of human rights should not be confused with criminal justice. [...] The objective of international human rights law is not to punish those individuals who are guilty of violations, but rather to protect the victims and to provide for the reparation of damages resulting from the acts of the States responsible.' (Inter-American Court of Human Rights, 1988).

18   Charles Cherno Jalloh, in his presentation at the 2014 CODESRIA conference, laments the 'unrealistic goals' set for criminal tribunals, including UNSC Res 1315(2000), which authorised the Special Court for Sierra Leone to call for 'a credible court that will contribute to peace, justice and reconciliation' (Wamae, 2014:7).

At the time of the rise of international criminal law and its controversies in the early 2000s, the African Court on Human and Peoples' Rights was gearing up for operationalisation. Its first bench was appointed in 2006. Equally, regional economic community (REC) courts were themselves coming to life. An amendment to the ECOWAS Treaty in 2005 granted the ECOWAS Community Court of Justice a human rights jurisdiction. The Tribunal of the Southern African Development Community, established in 1992, was inaugurated in 2005. The East African Court of Justice, established in 1999, was inaugurated in 2001. These African courts occasionally issued bold pro-victim decisions. Coupled with the new focus on human rights and abhorrence of mass atrocity evident in the Constitutive Act of the African Union, the 2000s held great promise for the concretisation of human rights protection and its victim-centred bias.

While the foregoing seeks not to challenge the currency of individual accountability for mass atrocity in the political economy of fighting impunity in Africa, as concerns victim-centredness, the sidelining of Africa's human rights system at its critical expansion phase would not have been helpful.

One clear opportunity for the future is the task of constructing an African human rights system that can effectively redress victims and advance the cause of accountability, usual[19] and manageable state resistance considered. The fund's origins and nomenclature, 'International Criminal Justice Fund', may have restricted its action to international criminal justice. Yet the central focus of this work – concern for the African victim of mass atrocity – calls on the fund, and indeed civil society, to at the very least consider the bird in hand as well as the two in the bush. It is testament to the fund's capacity to listen to its constituency and evolve, that in March 2016 it hosted a convening in Arusha, at the margins of the Ordinary Session of the African Court on Human and Peoples' Rights to precisely consider the role of human rights law in redressing victims of mass atrocities.

---

19   It is not unusual for states to resist and indeed defy international courts. The UK is currently (2016) defying the European Court of Human Rights demand for a repeal of a blanket ban on prisoner voting rights. The US defied the International Court of Justice's 1986 reparations demands for invading Nicaragua. Colombia withdrew from the ICJ's compulsory jurisdiction over its award of disputed islands to Nicaragua. The Inter-American Court of Human Rights has been defied by Trinidad and Tobago and Venezuela over the death penalty and judicial independence.

Conclusion

The fund has thus far succeeded in being nimble, risking to work outside the usual circuit of English-speaking African NGOs and promoting engagement in a wide array of aspects of atrocity accountability in Africa. It has also brought together the major grant makers to act in concert, and has provided a fresh and universally (among its donors and partners) welcome approach to grant making, proving that close and interested working relationships with partners need not threaten objectivity but rather provide for more intelligent grant making.

While leveraging Western donor resources, it has built a reputation of harmonising diverse interests, as was the vision of its founding donors. Its example demonstrates that donors having 'an agenda' does not necessarily mean that they act to the detriment of African agency. The fund's constituency (donors, grantees and other partners) laud the fund's value proposition and its contribution to the vision of a continent respectful of human rights and fighting impunity. Partners are universal in praising the fund's preparedness, its knowledge of local contexts, its willingness to listen to grantee perspectives and its proactive participation in preparation of grant seeking documentation.

The fund is not the first or only African grant maker, nor is it the only collaborative basket fund. It is not the only actor in international criminal justice, and is not the only one to seek out underserved communities in its field of work. In its first three years of operation, the fund has remained open to knowledge from the periphery, allowing its partners to influence its interventions and broadening its scope from solely supporting one institution to a range that is sensitive to each situation's peculiarities. The fund's successes need be seen from the point of view of its own origins and aims. Its example, being young and fully seizing the African right to act, even at the risk of making mistakes, still has a long way to go. However, it has begun forcefully.

In seeking out the unbeaten path, the fund has started to build up movements, and within these has encouraged the growth of NGOs with weak capacities. Its next task lies in appropriately determining its exit strategy from specific communities. It must remain long enough to achieve its aims and allow its partners to develop, but it must, as with all grant makers, avoid debilitating dependence.

So, what then is an authentic African response to the impunity for egregious human rights violations? African agency has always been multifaceted, complex and operating from a position of reference to Western resources. African philanthropy in the twenty-first century will be no different. Yet African agency has always evolved, its strength being not the right to make mistakes, but to learn from these mistakes and reanimate African faith in Africa rising. Atrocity accountability is among Africa's most potent debates today. It is fitting therefore that African agency, so described, is active here, as well.

References

Fanon, F. (1963) *Wretched of the Earth*. London, Penguin.

Gathii, J.T. (2011) 'The neo-liberal turn in regional trade agreements' *Washington Law Review*, 86 (3).

Inter-American Court of Human Rights (1988) *Velásquez Rodríguez v Honduras*, Judgment of 29 July 1988, (Ser. C) No. 4.

Jallow, H.B. (2012) *Journey for Justice*. Bloomington, AuthorHouse.

Mkapa, B.W. (2016) 'The role of African leaders in conflict resolution and peacebuilding', in J.R.Stormes SJ, E.O. Opongo SJ, K. Wansamo SJ and P. Knox SJ (eds), *Transitional Justice in Post-Conflict Societies in Africa*. Nairobi, Paulines Publications.

Nyerere, J.K. (1970) 'Non-Alignment in the 1970s: Opening Speech to the Preparatory Conference of the Non-Aligned Movement' 12 April.

Shivji, I.G. (2005) 'Silences in the NGO Discourse: The Role and Future of NGOs in Africa' Symposium on NGOs Keynote Address at the MS-Training Centre for Development Cooperation in Arusha, Tanzania, 28-29 November. Later republished as Shivji, I.G. (2007) *Silences in the NGO Discourse: The Role and Future of NGOs in Africa*. Nairobi, Fahamu Books.

TrustAfrica (2015) ICJ Fund Mid Term Evaluation Report (September), p. 13.

TrustAfrica and MacArthur Foundation (2011) Advancing International Criminal Justice in Africa: State Responsibility, the African Union and the International Criminal Court Report of Conference, 14-16 November 2011, Nairobi – Kenya, organised by Centre for Citizens' Participation on the African Union (CCP-AU), TrustAfrica and MacArthur Foundation.

Wamae, N. (2014) Conference Report, International Criminal Justice, Reconciliation and Peace in Africa: The ICC and Beyond, 10-12 July, Hotel Novotel Dakar.

4

A Grounded Approach to Philanthropy: Strengthening civil society in Liberia and Zimbabwe

Alice L. Brown

Introduction

TrustAfrica was established as a pan-African foundation focused on improving governance and development in Africa. While the organisation's founders valued constructive and mutually beneficial international cooperation, their underlying premise was that individuals and organisations on the continent had the capability to create, foster and implement African solutions to African problems. They were committed to counteracting the negative perceptions of Africa as a hopeless continent without agency and in perpetual need of oversight and assistance from external sources, primarily from the global north. In this way, TrustAfrica embodied a philosophy of African agency in a theory of change that views civic movement building as a catalyst for lasting social change. Accordingly, TrustAfrica strives to help develop an influential body of informed, networked, and durable civil society organisations (CSOs) that possess the capacity to hold governments and other power holders accountable to their respective citizenries.

This chapter focuses on TrustAfrica's efforts to support and strengthen civil society's work on democratic governance and accountability in two countries – Liberia and Zimbabwe – using the lenses of African agency and African philanthropy, reflecting on the extent to which the work enhanced African agency, asking if it has made a difference that it was led by an African-based philanthropy, and highlighting some key achievements and challenges in this regard.[1] Both programmes, the Liberian Civil Society Initiative (LCSI) and the Zimbabwe Alliance, were grounded in TrustAfrica's theory of change: they aimed to help build strong citizen movements of well-resourced and knowledgeable civil society actors able to conduct research, generate knowledge and advocate effectively. Activities were to include grant-making, knowledge generation, capacity building and strategic meetings, known as convenings, which were to serve as opportunities for networking and collaborative action. In both cases, the donors were motivated by the historical moment. As the following sections relate, each country was facing an important political period where democratic governance was at stake.

The Liberian Civil Society Initiative

With a population of approximately 4.4 million, Liberia is a country rich in natural resources, but it is one of the world's least developed countries, with approximately 85% of the population living below the international poverty line. For 14 years, Liberia was in the throes of two brutal civil wars (1989 to 1997 and 1999 to 2003) that cost the lives of an estimated 500,000 and displaced approximately one million others. In addition to death, displacement and destruction, these wars devastated Liberia's already feeble and struggling economy. To illustrate, before 1990 the mining sector contributed more than 65% of the country's export earnings and represented approximately 25% of GDP. During the war years, all major mines were closed and the sector's contribution to the economy became inconsequential (EITI, 2016).

In 2005, Liberia held its first post-conflict democratic election; Ellen Johnson Sirleaf became the country's first female president and the first woman to head an African state in modern times; she was re-elected in 2011. Since 2005, the Liberian government has made a number of advances with regard to good governance and transparency. These include efforts to strengthen or establish accountability institutions such as the

---

1   These issues have been interrogated through an examination of internal programme documents, external sources and the reflections and observations of TrustAfrica programme staff, funded partners and donor collaborators interviewed by the author.

Liberia Anti-Corruption Commission and the Public Procurement and Concessions Commissions. In addition, in 2009 Liberia obtained certification as Africa's first Extractive Industries Transparency Initiative (EITI)-compliant state. The Sirleaf administration has been generally supportive and protective of civil liberties such as freedom of speech and expression and access to information, establishing, for example, an Information Commission to handle information requests from the public. At the same time, the government has achieved a sizable increase in foreign direct investment. Government revenue from the extractive sector rose by more than 68% to US$186 million in fiscal year 2012/13, with the value of total commodity exports growing by 126% to $352 million (EITI, 2016).

These are all noteworthy accomplishments. Yet, the administration has faced numerous critical challenges, primary among these being ensuring stability in the country, stimulating broad economic growth and reviving democratic governance. Unemployment and illiteracy are endemic and corruption is rife, despite the presence of key accountability institutions. Public service reforms remain incomplete, with widespread allegations of nepotism and patronage, and although many public officials have been suspended or forced to resign due to allegations of corruption, there have been few prosecutions. Despite the various social responsibility portfolios of the leading concession companies, citizens lament the fact that resource extraction agreements rarely benefit their communities. All of these challenges were exacerbated by the Ebola outbreak that plagued the country from March 2014 until May 2015, severely affecting normal life and further weakening the economy (EITI, 2016).

In 2008, TrustAfrica and Humanity United joined in a partnership to strengthen civil society, recognising that intensified support for the sector could bolster Liberia's chances to move away from its recent brutal past. Over time, the effort was supplemented by an anonymous donor as well as from TrustAfrica's own core flexible funds. It must be noted here that the Liberian peace process had been helped in great part by the intervention of civil society actors who were a part of peace efforts. After the war, several factors combined to suggest a continuing and greater role for civil society. These included the fragility of the new peace project, the scale of efforts required to help take Liberia forward, and the importance of having independent voices holding the state accountable. At the same time, the sector had suffered greatly under the war and required significant institutional strengthening, sometimes at extremely basic levels. The peacetime project also required new skills, particularly around engaging at the policy level. Collaboration between Liberian civil society actors and the concentration of activities in the capital at the expense of rural communities were flagged as challenges to address.

Accordingly, the overarching goal of the LCSI was to encourage more accountable governance in the country by advancing and supporting policies to improve the circumstances of poor and vulnerable people. The objectives included: (i) bolstering the capacity of civil society to monitor national government and engage in advocacy; and (ii) empowering citizens to engage constructively with local authorities to develop their communities in a way that advanced inclusive governance. In addition, the LCSI sought to promote professional media practice focused on investigative journalism targeting critical areas of governance. Between 2008 and 2015, the LCSI supported 35 institutions via 81 grants, disbursing more than $4.7 million. The approach of the LCSI has been to support the substantive and technical capacity of its partners, funding thematic interventions and enabling a combination of tailored trainings and convenings on institutional strengthening, policy, advocacy and research. Following the first phase of the LCSI, it was recognised that more tailored capacity building and institutional support was needed, and TrustAfrica adapted its training interventions accordingly.[2] The LCSI is currently in its third phase, which has seen further consolidation, as well as a recognition that while overall gains are being made, resources are too limited and diversely spread to have a concentrated impact on any particular one area. Hence the LCSI is now focusing on helping CSOs in their efforts to monitor the extractives industry in Liberia, and to raise their collective voices.

It can be difficult to isolate impact and attribute it to a specific intervention such as LCSI. Yet, observations by staff and partners indicate some broad gains. First, institutions that have been repeat grantees have become more adept at conceptualising and implementing quality research. Second, several partners have honed community mobilisation skills. Third, a critical mass of TrustAfrica-funded CSOs are now linking local community empowerment initiatives to larger challenges within Liberian policy environment. Fourth, thematic area specialisation, including research, is becoming entrenched at several TrustAfrica-funded

---

2   An in-depth and tailored capacity-building intervention was designed in partnership with West African Civil Society Institute.

groups. Finally, LCSI thematic area or project collaborations have enhanced other CSO networks.

Other notable accomplishments cited in partner interviews and reports include the contribution of LCSI partners to the development of Liberia's first Media Assistance Strategy and a Media Quality Barometer, which defines areas for media development and assesses the performance of leading media establishments on a regular basis.[3] The Initiative's support for the advocacy of the Press Union of Liberia and other media organisations led to the passage of the Freedom of Information Act of 2010, an important advance for press freedom and public accountability. Support also enabled Actions for Genuine Democratic Alternatives (Agenda), an LCSI partner working with Civicus, to develop Liberia's first Civil Society Index, which looks at capacity constraints and local perceptions of civil society. It is worth noting that Agenda, a nascent institution at the time, has emerged as one of the leading CSOs on research and policy in Liberia. Other support enabled youth to participate in governance processes within three counties and helped strengthen conflict resolution initiatives in Liberia's most ethnically diverse county. Policy-related achievements included convenings with high-level policymakers to enable civil society input and activities to establish mechanisms to monitor and prevent election-related violence.

More recently, the LCSI established the Concessions Working Group (CWG), a diverse coalition that serves as a clearing house for on-going discussions and advocacy on natural resource governance within Liberia. The CWG launched various advocacy campaigns to bring attention to human rights violations against citizens in concession areas, including forced evictions, unlawful land-grabs and death threats. The group provided vital reporting to the Independent National Human Rights Commission of Liberia on gross rights violations in the extractives sector. In the policy arena, the LCSI has enabled critical feedback to the Land Commission on Liberia's new land law, emphasising a community human rights perspective for land tenure. The CWG has also put forward civil society's positions on current concessions agreements in strategic meetings with the chair of the House of Senate Standing Committee on Concessions at the Liberia legislature. The Initiative has created and

---

3   During the launch of the second quarterly barometer, Liberian Vice President Joseph Boakai expressed gratitude to the Liberia Media Center, an LCSI partner, and TrustAfrica for what he termed a 'great step towards the professionalism and critical introspection within the Liberian media'.

maintained productive relationships with various departments within the Liberian government, in particular with the National Investment Commission, the National Bureau of Concessions and the Forestry Department, contributing in part to enabling more inclusive, transparent and accountable governance processes. Finally, the work of the LCSI has been amplified through strategic partnerships with other influential civil society groups, including the Liberia Extractives Industries Transparency Initiative, Publish What You Pay Liberia and the Liberia Peace Building Office.

The Zimbabwe Alliance

After decades of colonial subjugation and a 15-year civil war, the Republic of Zimbabwe was established in 1980, having gained independence from white minority rule. Today, this Southern African country has a population of approximately 14 million people. Robert Mugabe, liberation leader and head of the Zimbabwe African National Union (ZANU, later ZANU-PF), was first elected prime minister in 1980 and then, in 1987 with an amendment to the constitution, he consolidated power as executive president. In office for the last 36 years, President Mugabe is one of the longest-serving African heads of state and the world's oldest.

Initially, during the 1980s and much of the 1990s, the newly independent nation prospered and various indices associated with its Human Development Index improved. Amongst other improvements, there was positive economic growth, agricultural production in abundance, impressive increases in the rates of adult literacy and one of the most robust health systems in the region (Murisa and Chikweche, 2015). Circumstances began to change, however, in the mid to late 1990s as one of Africa's most promising economies began to spiral into an economic meltdown that lasted almost a decade. The contributing factors were multifaceted, complex and contentious. Amongst others, Zimbabwe was hard hit by the HIV pandemic which, by 1999, was claiming the lives of approximately 1,500 Zimbabweans a week (ibid.). Agricultural production was adversely affected by severe droughts and, in 2000, the controversial Fast Track Land Reform Programme, which involved the seizure and redistribution of white-owned commercial farms, was promulgated. Accompanying all of this was widespread and devastating hardship: unemployment and poverty increased, agricultural production and exports fell into sharp decline, food shortages kicked in, social unrest in the form of protests and strikes became common place, outward migration rose, and political strife and repression grew. The economy began to fall in 2000, reaching an astronomical hyperinflation rate of 11,200,000% by 2008. In a nutshell, Zimbabwe was in crisis.

As keenly observed by Murisa and Chikweche (2015: xiii), 'Whilst the causes of the crisis remains a topic of debate, its negative impact on … politics, the economy and the general social fabric (inclusive of welfare and social services delivery) cannot be disputed.' Indeed, according to the World Bank (2016), 'the political and economic crises that characterized the economy between 2000 and 2008 contributed to the nearly halving of its GDP … and raising poverty rates of more than 72%, with over a fifth of the population in extreme poverty. Health, education and other basic services, once regional models, largely collapsed and Zimbabwe's Human Development Index (HDI) in 2011 stood at 173 out of 187 countries'.

During this same period, President Mugabe and the ZANU-PF ruling party were accused of becoming increasingly authoritarian, corrupt and disdainful of the rights of citizens. Many Zimbabweans began to question and challenge policies, the lack of leadership change and the entrenchment of a de facto one-party state. In 1999, the opposition Movement for Democratic Change (MDC) was formed and, along with various CSOs, confronted the hegemony of ZANU-PF. The state responded with intimidation, a crack-down on civil liberties and force. Parliamentary and presidential elections held from the late 1990s to 2008 were marred by state-sponsored violence, and were seriously flawed and widely viewed as having been manipulated by the ruling party.

In September 2008, ZANU-PF and the MDC agreed to form an inclusive government based on a negotiated Global Political Agreement (GPA). The parties agreed to share power and jointly undertake a constitutional reform process geared to creating the conditions for free and fair elections. This political settlement, combined with the adoption of a multi-currency regime (that is, the dollarising of the economy) in 2009, allowed Zimbabwe to embark on a period of stabilisation and avert an imminent collapse of the state. According to TrustAfrica staff, however, within a year the political situation had been replaced by 'increased political polarisation, escalating cases of political violence and political arrests, a near collapse of the constitutional reform process, and virtual collapse of the GPA'. Fragmented, under threat and in an environment of limited resources and shrinking civic and political space, civil society's role was in urgent need of additional support, financial and otherwise.

TrustAfrica began to engage in efforts to respond to the crisis in Zimbabwe in 2007. Two years later, in light of the brutalisation of civil society and abuses to democratic processes, it joined with like-minded donors to create the Zimbabwe Alliance. The Alliance included TrustAfrica, the Wallace Global Fund, the Schooner Foundation and the International Development Exchange (IDEX).[4] With a secretariat staffed by TrustAfrica, decision-making is taken jointly. The mandate of the Alliance is to strengthen civil society and promote human rights and democracy in Zimbabwe.[5] In the context of the fluid political dynamics and the constitutional reform process and elections required by its terms, these donors saw a unique opportunity to support Zimbabwe's transition to democracy by helping to strengthen the country's civil society and civic participation. Constitutional reform and the promotion of free and fair elections thus emerged as key goals in the immediate term, with medium to longer-term goals revolving around strengthening civil society and social movements to promote informed and effective citizen participation and to secure democratic rights and civil liberties. Included in this was the aim of ensuring that marginalised groups, particularly women, were not left behind. Participants recognised that civil society would need to be rebuilt if it were to contribute effectively to Zimbabwe's socio-economic and political transformation. Against this backdrop, the Zimbabwe Alliance initially focused on the three strategic priorities: (i) strengthening the community and constituency base of civil society; (ii) strengthening the intellectual and knowledge base of civil society; and (iii) strengthening national coordination and advocacy.

The Zimbabwe Alliance organised consultative meetings with civil society partners and other key actors on the situation in the country with a particular focus on civil society responses.[6] During the constitutional reform process, its work contributed to greater civil society coordination and increased public participation. It also ensured that the focus of reforms went beyond civil liberties to include social and economic rights. Significantly, this work directly informed the content of

4   Prior to this a loose collaboration had existed in a different and more limited form. In 2009 an expanded funding and management configuration emerged, now involving TrustAfrica and others. This discussion deals only with activities in the post-2009 period.

5   Since its inception the Zimbabwe Alliance has also received support from other sources, including the Mize Family Trust, the Lester Fund, the American Jewish World Service and individual contributors.

6   Participants included the Crisis in Zimbabwe Coalition, ZimRights, Bulawayo Progressive Residents Association, Amandla Center, and the Magamba Network.

the new constitution through a technical team that the Alliance funded to support the drafting process. The result included provisions related to greater accountability, political rights and civil liberties. In March 2013, the proposed constitution was endorsed by 95% of voters in a national referendum.

Despite the best efforts of the Zimbabwe Alliance and other like-minded groups and individuals, the country did not realise an undisputed free and fair election in 2013. It did, however, contribute to a stronger, more skilled and more viligant civil society, capacitated with the skills and knowledge to monitor and report on the activities of government. Specifically, the Elections Watch project that Zimbabwe Alliance co-created in partnership with Hivos-IMS and several CSOs was one of the most extensive collaborative elections monitoring projects ever established in the country. The project itself was unprecedented in terms of utilising new ICTs and mobile phone technology through Ushahidi, a platform that interconnected a nationwide network of election monitors and enabled real-time reporting of election-related incidents and violations via a special website that Zimbabwe Alliance developed. Using this platform, election monitors were alerted to incidents and able to organise timely interventions. The expectation was that this would help create an environment more conducive to free and fair elections.

The Zimbabwe Alliance has made 36 grants to 19 institutions working on strengthening civil society and promoting democracy. These include assisting civil society participation in crucial political processes, such as constitutional reform and elections, while simultaneously enhancing the capacity of key CSOs, activists and policymakers to participate in those processes. It also helped amplify voices of traditionally marginalised groups, especially artists, women and community based organisations (CBOs) and created platforms for civil society to engage in dialogue and to coordinate strategies. Importantly, the Alliance provided urgent support and protection to human rights defenders facing dangerous circumstances and mobilised regional and international solidarity in support of constitutional reform and democratic processes, extending its work to Zimbabwe's diaspora and facilitating their participation in shaping the future of the country. Finally, the Zimbabwe Alliance facilitated peer learning and coordination among donors working in Zimbabwe.

More recently, as part of its contribution to thought leadership on social and political transformation, the Zimbabwe Alliance facilitated the establishment of a research group comprising civil society actors and university-based activist academics who produced papers to inform discussion and action on various aspects of Zimbabwe's social, economic and political transformation. Some of these papers became chapters in *Beyond the Crises: Zimbabwe's Prospects for Transformation,* a book published by Weaver Press and TrustAfrica in 2015. The Alliance also convened several discussions to catalyse youth to promote democracy and social change in Zimbabwe, offered skills training and workshops regarding use of ICTs in monitoring service delivery and the political environment, and invested in efforts to strengthen CBOs through resident's forums.

Process is critical to impact: The value add of the Liberian Civil Society Initiative and the Zimbabwe Alliance

TrustAfrica's theory of change centres on supporting a critical mass of networked and resilient civil society organisations as a key strategy for enabling public and private accountability, and thus a reduction in injustices. In Liberia and Zimbabwe, TrustAfrica's support enabled significant gains. This next section takes a closer look at the process of providing support and the extent to which the nature of TrustAfrica's support enabled agency for movement building. Were marginalised voices included in its programming? What did groups find valuable about the nature of the support given? Did it make a difference that TrustAfrica was an Africa-based donor led by Africans?

This reflection finds that in both Liberia and Zimbabwe, TrustAfrica has (i) enhanced the capacity of key CSOs, activists and policymakers, and amplified the voices of traditionally marginalised groups; (ii) created platforms for civil society to engage in dialogue and to coordinate strategies; and (iii) facilitated peer learning and coordination among donors. To ensure that solutions were indeed informed and driven by those most affected, TrustAfrica facilitated collaborative fora and helped build the administrative, technical and substantive capacity of CSOs. The way in which TrustAfrica engaged with its partners was universally acknowledged and valued by funded partners and donor partners, who highlighted several critical factors about TrustAfrica's approach.

A grounded partner: The fact that TrustAfrica is an African institution with local staff who have deep understanding of the contexts and changing dynamics was seen as a critical factor in how the organisation operates. One partner observed that far too many donors, especially large bilateral and multilateral funders, make decisions at a distance through remote requests for proposals processes. As a result, these funders are often disengaged from groups and activities 'on the ground'. TrustAfrica's local presence and rootedness was seen as a key factor enabling active engagement with partners including discussing ideas, sharing perspectives and providing feedback through concept notes and proposal drafting steps, all grounded in a process of 'agreement around ideas'. Another representative cited this approach to grant making as the 'singular difference' between TrustAfrica and other donors. Indeed, TrustAfrica, with its fulltime presence in Liberia and Zimbabwe, has been able to keep abreast of developments, build intimate relationships with like-minded entities and respond quickly to opportunities as they arise. Its position on the frontlines allows it to be an integral part of the strategising and co-creation of solutions alongside civil society and other democratic actors. The role of TrustAfrica goes beyond funding, to an active involvement in strengthening democracy in Liberia and Zimbabwe.

Beyond grant making: TrustAfrica combined grants and technical assistance in a way that enabled groups to both increase effectiveness and attract additional resources. To one partner, it was a 'great mix' because it helped build the internal capacity of local groups. TrustAfrica often commissioned consultants and other service providers to assist emerging or nascent CSOs to strengthen their organisational capacity. In other words, TrustAfrica helped fill gaps with regard to strategic planning, institutional development and financial management. Then, direct grant assistance followed. Over the course of two to three years, the twinning of technical assistance and grant support 'really helped' this organisation. In fact, it gave it the ability to attract additional resources from elsewhere and to decrease its financial dependence on TrustAfrica. The CEO spoke highly of this 'unique aspect of the interaction with TrustAfrica' and suggested that this 'should be copied by other donors'.

A holistic approach to institutional strengthening: For too long, initiatives aimed at organisational development have focused solely on administrative elements – building sound boards, good governance, fundraising, financial management and the like. While these are critical to building strong institutions, they create an architecture that supports competence without focusing on programmatic impact. The value of TrustAfrica's approach is that over and above the administrative and technical support, it has also focused on the substantive elements through broad-based convenings that enable interrogation of ideas and strategies; through workshops on critical skills such as policy advocacy and research; and by catalysing the generation of new knowledge to enable appropriate interventions. In Liberia, for instance, one partner explained that through its partnership with TrustAfrica, it 'internalised' an understanding of taxation, transfer pricing, tax resourcing and compliance that it had not had previously. At the time of research, the organisation was about to enter into a memorandum of understanding to assist the Liberian Revenue Authority with developing tax policies related to natural resources management in the country, thus ensuring that civil society voices and perspectives would be represented as this essential department goes about its work. Hence, the skills acquisition not only strengthened this CSO but also enabled the organisation to contribute tangibly to enhanced government performance and accountability. This partner representative explained that this is a tremendous development for the organisation and credits TrustAfrica with having the insight to support such technical and substantive capacity building.

Supporting new and diverse voices: TrustAfrica's programme strategy documents reflect a dedication to amplifying marginalised voices. For instance, the Liberia strategy statement for 2008-2010 explicitly stated that it would consider only programmes that cover at least two counties or that are community centered in the sense that they seek to empower rural or remote communities. It also required that partners work with local groups, whether formal or informal, as long as the said groups have constituencies of their own. Feedback reflects that TrustAfrica progressed well on its mandate to include marginalised voices: a common observation amongst partners in both locations was that TrustAfrica has helped new, fledgling organisations start, develop and evolve into important actors on the civil society scene. Partners spoke highly of the ability and willingness of TrustAfrica to provide seed funding for new ideas and projects and to help them attract additional support from diverse sources as they developed. The implications of this can be seen in the role that these additional voices from the margins have played in both countries.

TrustAfrica's collaborative approach in particular was instrumental in identifying promising groups that brought new voices to the fore. For example, the Zimbabwe Alliance helped to amplify historically marginalised groups through support for youth collectives such as the Magamba Cultural Activist Network, a prominent collective promoting the vision of a free and just Zimbabwe through creative youth activism, new media, popular cultural events and citizen journalism. By supporting Magamba in its initial stages, the Zimbabwe Alliance helped it to build its name and reputation such that it has become 'one of the leading creative organisations in the country' able to attract further support from other sponsors. Further, TrustAfrica adopts an inclusive approach that not only funds the participation of its partners but also supports the involvement of organisations that are not financially supported by it. This is seen as extremely valuable in bringing different perspectives to the table.

The value of collaborative fora: TrustAfrica's enabling of collaborative fora was highlighted as an important strategy and contribution. In both countries, partners worked together through collective platforms such as networks and coalitions, efforts that not only enhanced coordination, but strengthened the collective voice of civil society. Partners appreciated TrustAfrica's ability to fund the infrastructure needed to create these platforms for civil society engagement and specifically noted the importance of connecting local NGOs and CBOs in collaborations and partnerships. In Liberia, for example, such efforts included the support of LCSI for the collective activities of the Concessions Working Group. TrustAfrica's ongoing support has enabled monthly meetings where organisations have been able to discuss key issues, share knowledge and information, plan advocacy campaigns and forge partnerships. The funding and facilitation provided by TrustAfrica have been critical to the success and continued existence of this group. In another example, the Zimbabwe Alliance convened several major players in Zimbabwean civil society to establish an extensive network to monitor elections and respond to violations. Immediately after the 2013 elections, the Alliance also partnered with the Open Society Initiative for Southern Africa (OSISA) and Heinrich Böll Stiftung (HBS) to convene the first major national conference for civil society to reflect on the agenda for social, economic and political transformation in Zimbabwe and to strategise for the future. TrustAfrica has continued the partnership with OSISA and HBS through the Zimbabwe Donors Convening that facilitates peer learning and promotes collaboration amongst donors working in Zimbabwe.

As pointed out in the interviews for this chapter, many collective activities and partnerships begin but fail to last because there is no secretariat or facilitator to follow up on decisions, organise meetings and generally keep matters on track. The fact that this work was able to continue in both countries was seen as a result of the unique role that TrustAfrica plays as an African philanthropy with close ties to the local context. It is noteworthy that TrustAfrica recognised this need and has been willing to invest in such support, in contrast to many funders that do not. This is in part because many donors focus primarily on quantifiable outputs as opposed to processes, such as building and strengthening agency, autonomy, independence and self-reliance.

Moreover, funders as well as partners gained value in collaborating. TrustAfrica's efforts to facilitate peer learning and coordination among donors were enhanced by the fact that although it is rooted on the continent it has the ability to act as an interlocutor with institutions in the global north. In speaking of the formal and informal ways in which the Zimbabwe Alliance facilitated ideas and actions amongst funders, for instance, one donor partner said that the 'convening power of TrustAfrica needs to be celebrated' while another spoke of its 'great intellectual partnership' with TrustAfrica. One partner commended the donor collaborative for being 'open to different ideas and proposals' and for being flexible and allowing objectives and aims to change over time. Ideas would be considered for funding if they fit within the overall goals, and this was a welcome contrast to 'other, more traditional funders'. In both Zimbabwe and Liberia, donors reported that working in concert ultimately resulted in better funding strategies, and enabled them to enhance efficiency and impact by avoiding duplication and fragmentation.

While collaboration poses its own challenges (as will be seen in the following section) both funders and partners acknowledged that working together made it possible to leverage limited resources and achieve collectively what would not have been possible through individual efforts.

Critical challenges and recommendations

The challenge of maintaining healthy collaboratives

The collaborations discussed in this chapter have yielded significant and substantial impacts. The processes of collaboration, however, are not always smooth. Several drawbacks and limitations bear reflection and yield important lessons not just for TrustAfrica but for donor collaboratives and partnerships in general.

Attention to the process: It can difficult and time-consuming to take decisions as a group, particularly if participants are located in different regions or countries. Moreover, collaborative arrangements, and the institutions that comprise them, are not static. Thus partners should periodically re-examine their goals, mission and principles for participation to evaluate whether they remain as defined at the onset or need to be revisited. This focus on process may seem counter-intuitive – requiring even more time – but it can provide important stability. Seeking clarity on goals, especially where contexts are fluid, can prevent misalignments and misunderstandings amongst and between the partners. As one donor partner observed, the substantive grant making of a collaborative can be on target, but if the processes and procedures essential to nurturing the collaboration itself are neglected, it can result in a loss of vitality, and atrophy. Periodic deliberation and review of processes and procedures is essential to the health and productivity of a partnership.

Good communication between partners: It is not uncommon for conflicts or tensions to arise around issues of control, especially if partners bring unequal resources to the table. Resentment can become an issue if one or two of the partners end up taking on the majority of the work. Differences due to individual or institutional egos, if not acknowledged or tended to, can become destructive and drain members' time and energy away from substantive issues such as programme strategy. Relationships within collaborations and partnerships should be supported and administered but also be actively prioritised and maintained.

Reconciling different cultural or institutional approaches: Members of collaboratives, whether of donors or funded partners, tend to have diverse backgrounds. This is especially true for those seeking to bring new voices to the fore, as was the case in both Liberia and Zimbabwe. As Briggs Bomba (2014) has observed, such diversity can result in 'a cultural or systems clash': 'This is revealed in many ways: for instance, a more deliberative approach to an issue in contrast to an expeditious one, inevitably creating a sense of one party feeling rushed and another feeling slowed down.' Donors differ in the size of the grants they want to make, or they may have a different approach to working with funded partners. TrustAfrica staff and others have found that good facilitation is one way to reconcile these differences.

Recognising the life cycle of the partnership: Whilst maintaining momentum and preserving the raison d'être is crucial for effectiveness, it is also critical to recognise when it makes sense to bring a collaboration to an end. This natural life cycle can be affected by external factors, such as change of legal regime or the onset of hostilities, and can even lead to premature mortality. Time-bound events, such as the post-2005 election situation in Liberia or the 2011 referendum on the new constitution in Zimbabwe, can provide a powerful rationale for a joint effort. But donors and partners should also closely consider what happens in the aftermath of that galvanising event or circumstance. The stimulus, energy and momentum created in response to these exceptional circumstances may dissipate in their aftermath. Other factors may include 'donor fatigue', or a change in priorities on the part of one or more partners. It makes sense therefore to pay attention to the appropriate lifespan of certain collaborations or partnerships and whether the strategic imperative of the work continues to be relevant in a changing context. It may be unrealistic and impractical to expect some joint efforts to survive much beyond the particular event or campaign that brought them into existence.

Addressing the sustainability issue: For a foundation such as TrustAfrica, which aims to sustain civil society in the long term, it is important to recognise that when a collaborative ends, so does the support to the funded partners. Their advocacy activities may therefore cease. Indeed, one staff member observed that 'good partners and initiatives can die off at the expiration of the project period because there is no investment in the sustainability of institutions.' Over time staff learnt to use the few resources they had 'to invest in partners' own operational and survival needs'. It will be important for TrustAfrica and others who fund civil society to ensure that capacity building work is undertaken with an eye towards strengthening the ability of organisations to increase their skills and influence during the grant period, and ultimately, to sustain their work beyond that period.

Ensuring a strong, equal voice for partners: From the perspective of civil society organisations, it may be important to engage in a more critical review of donor-inspired collaborations and partnerships. While collaboration at this level may enhance efficiency, strengthen strategies and avoid duplication of efforts, the manner in which a donor introduces a collaborative model to a collective of funded partners can also be problematic and even non-productive. Donor-dictated collaborations between partners may undermine institutional autonomy and thwart the growth of African agency. A process that has not been sufficiently inclusive can result in unintended consequences, including the suppression of marginalised or vulnerable voices, such as those of women and youth, within the collective. Donors and potential partners might ask: Has a partnership been created organically, out of genuine consultative processes, or is it a forced marriage between reluctant parties?

The challenge of representation and women's leadership

The LCSI and the Zimbabwe Alliance are committed to promoting the agency of African voices, especially the least empowered and most marginalised such as women and youth. Yet in both initiatives there is an overwhelming presence of the male voice in leadership positions. This, despite the best intentions of TrustAfrica, which promotes women's rights and gender equality and funds women-led and women-focused CSOs as well as capacity building for women. Still, it appears that these voices have not been absorbed into the leadership of the governance and democracy programming in Liberia and Zimbabwe. Why is this so, especially given the commitment of TrustAfrica to agency, equality and empowerment? In partial response to this inquiry, one TrustAfrica staff observed that although TrustAfrica aims to lift up marginalised voices, and has done so in some instances in the context of youth, 'no specific gender lens has been developed to guide this type of intervention'. Another staff member reflects that 'Though we've managed to fund a few women-focused outfits in Liberia, the programmatic lens has not necessarily been about women's issues and I think this is something we should be doing considering our mantra on African agency.'

This critique considers that TrustAfrica's programming in Liberia and Zimbabwe may be undertaken in a manner that does not easily lend itself to including women's representation and diversity issues. If, for instance, the thematic lens of a programme is on democracy and governance-related issues, then the focus would concentrate on elections and related processes. This narrow focus, concedes one staff member, might not necessarily include 'women's rights per se' and may have resulted in missed opportunities. What's more, this sometimes constricting definition of programmatic areas 'is an issue across the institution'.

This dynamic played out, staff observed, in an agenda concentrated too narrowly on elections, a focus that may well have prevented the integration of women and diversity issues into the programme. Further, there may have been insufficient questions and conversations within the programme with regard to pushing a gender analysis. By way of illustration, TrustAfrica requires all funded partners to include their diversity profiles as part of the application process, but this may have become a perfunctory exercise rather than a meaningful exploration of the power and gender dynamics within a particular organisation and the need to challenge these dynamics. This diversity inquiry needs to be 'deepened'.

This could indicate the TrustAfrica may need to pause and reflect on what aspects of its programmatic approach need to change in order to take on a more substantive gender character to its work. Without question, the political commitment is there, but with respect to the operationalisation of promoting the representation of women and gender parity, the programmatic interventions may not have been sufficient. In terms of lessons learned from the first ten years of practice, perhaps this discussion demonstrates the need for TrustAfrica to place a greater emphasis on mainstreaming gender and diversity issues into all its programmes.

It must be stressed, however, that mainstreaming is not an end in itself but a strategy, a means, to achieve a goal. In this instance, the goal would centre on promoting and advancing gender equity and the agency of women. Specifically, mainstreaming here would involve ensuring that women's participation, perspective and voice find a more prominent place amongst CSOs and movements focused on democracy and governance. Mainstreaming should not usurp or diminish the need for targeted interventions aimed at supporting women-led and women-focused initiatives. Indeed, the two are not mutually exclusive: TrustAfrica may want to consider a more assertive approach to mainstreaming the representation of women in these CSOs while continuing to maintain, expand and enhance its targeted interventions aimed at strengthening women-led and women-focused groups. This Achilles heel is not exclusive to TrustAfrica. Democracy and governance funders, as well as civil society itself, needs to take special measures to ensure the promotion of women's leadership and voice within traditionally male-dominated CSOs.

It needs to be emphasised that the best intentions of social justice donors often come face to face with the stark reality of societal norms and culture that perpetuate patriarchy and male dominance. To be sure, the progressive ideals of some donors and CSOs clash with pre-existing prejudices, biases, apathy, reluctance or resistance. Thus it may take longer to measure the impact and progress of efforts to promote women's leadership. It may take longer than progressive-minded donors anticipate to see the presence of women in leadership positions in CSOs focused on governance and democracy. Donor attempts to tip the scales in favour of equity and alter the balance of power are essential, but it must be understood that these processes and transformations require continuous, constant, evolving and long-term interventions.

The challenge of being a philanthropy that both gives funds and receives funds

TrustAfrica is an institution that both makes and receives grants. How does this dual identity influence the agency of TrustAfrica itself? The challenges and tensions dictate some constraints on its ability to make unilateral decisions on such issues as the focus of its grant making, what and whom to fund, the longevity of grants and strategies, the periods of time over which to fund certain campaigns or interventions and whether and how to assist its partners in addressing issues of sustainability.

For instance, TrustAfrica may desire to set up a rapid response fund or a dedicated endowed fund to strengthen the sustainability and longevity of CSOs in Liberia and Zimbabwe. Yet, as a recipient of donor funds, TrustAfrica is bound by the grant agreements with its own donors that may not allow for these types of funding vehicles. Just as its partners must comply with the mandates of TrustAfrica, so too must TrustAfrica abide by the requirements of its grantors. As such, when partners in the two programmes lament the fact that TrustAfrica (along with other donors) tends to provide project-based and short-term funding,[7] one wonders how this could be different given the reality of TrustAfrica's own funding constraints. As one staff member noted, 'Funding streams for organisations such as TrustAfrica are not unrestricted.' As a result, TrustAfrica may be restricted in its ability to establish certain funding structures that it deems optimal. Although it certainly has some independent agency, TrustAfrica does not have complete or sole authority to

7 A number of Liberian and Zimbabwean funded partners expressed that TrustAfrica, along with other donors, tends to provide project-based and short-term funding. These representatives spoke of the ways in which such a funding approach constrains progress, momentum and continuity. One representative pointed out that because TrustAfrica funds its activities and programmes on a project-basis for a period of one year, or perhaps two, at a time, the NGO finds it difficult to recruit and retain qualified, motivated staff as employee contracts must reflect the funding limits. Due to this insecurity, when longer term, more stable and secure employment opportunities are offered, many staff members accept them, resulting in a loss of momentum and institutional memory for the NGO or CBO on the ground and adversely impacting the progress of the intervention and general staff morale.

disperse funds as it may desire.

Nevertheless, the dual identity of TrustAfrica holds some advantages. As an African-based philanthropy established, in its initial stages, with monies from northern donors, TrustAfrica has had continued access not only to financial resources but also to technical assistance and professional guidance from those sources. Likewise, these funders have also benefitted from their relationship with TrustAfrica, which serves as an intellectual resource helping them to better understand the various African contexts. This has enabled northern donors to make more informed decisions with regard to their philanthropy. TrustAfrica has advised them on critical gaps and helped them facilitate different types of relationships with NGOs and CBOs on the ground. Hence, the dual identity of TrustAfrica allows for mutually beneficial and supportive relationships between it and external donors.

Looking outward, TrustAfrica, both as grantee and grantor, has earned the trust and respect of funders originating in the global north as demonstrated by the support received and the multiple partnerships and collaborations forged. Looking inward, as an African-based philanthropy, TrustAfrica has extensive connections to CSOs in various parts of the continent and, as a consequence, it has its institutional finger on the pulse of pressing and current issues facing the citizens of various African nations. TrustAfrica is indeed well placed to discuss these issues and circumstances with donors and other interested parties, from both the global north and the global south. Moreover, it acts as an intermediary between larger donors and small to medium size CSOs on the continent that may have difficulty accessing funds from global and international sources. Likewise, it performs an important role for larger donors who are restricted and limited in their ability to directly reach and support these locally-based institutions.

TrustAfrica's dual identity has at times inhibited its ability to help build a critical mass of informed, networked, and resilient CSOs capable of holding governments accountable. Yet it has found other ways to advance this aim, for instance by acting as an advocate and a facilitator, forging relationships and providing support that goes beyond its role as grantee and grantor. One example is the case of the Institute for Young Women Development (IYWD), a self-described 'young feminist organisation.'[8] Although the Zimbabwe Alliance was not in a position to

---

8   'IYWD is committed to mobilising and strengthening the voice and power of young women in marginalised communities to transform the status quo through

fund IYWD, staff introduced this dynamic group to IDEX which provided IYWD with support and is now developing a long-term relationship with the group.

This is just one example of a way in which Zimbabwe Alliance, and by extension, TrustAfrica, acts as a connector[9] and fills an important role in the context of helping to (i) build organisations and movements that are the catalysts for lasting social change and (ii) promote diversity and transformation within civil society in Zimbabwe. Similarly, one Liberia-based partner described TrustAfrica as 'more than a donor, it is an enabler'.

Wearing both these hats, TrustAfrica has, in the context of the LCSI and the Zimbabwe Alliance, played a number of roles and served a variety of functions that have contributed to the success of these collaborations. In both countries the work has advanced civil society's ability to influence policy, with specific achievements. Moving forward, TrustAfrica should look to maximise and capitalise on these. Given its dual identity and its track record since its establishment in 2006, TrustAfrica is ideally placed to help carve out space for experimenting with new ways to address CSO sustainability in Africa. Indeed, the need to invest in the sustainability of institutions and initiatives is an important lesson that TrustAfrica staff have come to learn and appreciate.

As it continues to strive to fulfil its mission and mandate of advancing African agency, TrustAfrica and other such donors face a dilemma: how to sustain support for civil society in a meaningful way when funding for such work is irregular? There is a need for more exploration of ways to use limited resources so that their benefits outlast the project time-frame. How can short-term capacity building be directed in a way that leaves the civil society organisation or network stronger in the long term?

TrustAfrica might also do more to create new streams of funding for this work. One avenue would be to dedicate attention and resources to

---

various programmes that engage communities, institutions and the young women themselves so that issues that marginalise and oppress them are eliminated.' From https://iywd.wordpress.com/what-we-do/.

9   Gladwell defined a connector as a person '...with a special gift for bringing the world together' (Gladwell, 2000: 38). Yet, 'Connectors are important for more than simply the number of people they know. Their importance is also a function of the kinds of people they know' (ibid.: 46). Although Gladwell wrote about individuals, the description could easily apply to an organisation such as TrustAfrica, which knows the global and international donor world and the African civil society sector and has displayed a gift for bringing them together.

attracting support and contributions from within the continent – appealing to the growing number of high net-worth individuals and other philanthropic endeavours indigenous to the African continent and the global south. Indeed, a major component of TrustAfrica's mandate, but one that has not received the attention required, is to leverage African philanthropic resources to minimise reliance on external donors.

Concluding remarks

The work of TrustAfrica, through the Liberia Civil Society Initiative and the Zimbabwe Alliance, has been an important contributor to the advancement of African agency. It has enabled institutions and individuals to conceptualise and implement what they have seen as the solutions to their challenges. While these initiatives have produced some constructive results – including several policy wins – in the short and medium term, it is too early to speak of long-term implications. Nonetheless, through the reflections and observations of TrustAfrica staff, partners and donors, and an emerging body of evidence, the work in Zimbabwe and Liberia illustrates at least in part TrustAfrica's theory of change: that a critical mass of informed, networked, and resilient CSOs can hold governments to account. TrustAfrica has indeed influenced and contributed to advancing critical social justice issues in Zimbabwe and Liberia, and it continues to do so.

Moreover, TrustAfrica has done this work with a vision and mandate that value and promote African agency and empowerment. The comments and insights of those consulted for this chapter affirm this, even as they offered a critical review of the work of TrustAfrica, bringing challenges and missed opportunities into the foreground. The fact that TrustAfrica grapples with these knotty, perplexing, unpredictable and often seemingly intractable issues within complicated and fluid contexts is an indication that it is fully engaged with the realities of the practice of social justice philanthropy on the African continent, and is committed to the promotion of agency, self-sufficiency, equality and democratic development.

Despite all of its progress, TrustAfrica – and other philanthropies seeking to promote social justice and democratic, accountable governance – must navigate political, economic and social terrains that can be volatile and unpredictable. They must deal with unequal power dynamics on a number of fronts, with their donors and in the contexts in which they work. They must negotiate cultural sensitivities and differences and address issues of sustainability for their funded partners while, in many cases, themselves being vulnerable to funding flows and the constraints that these place on them.

It is therefore vital to have a critical interrogation of the expectations that are placed on such institutions, particularly if they are being seen as nodes for enabling agency through philanthropy. Any long-term success in advancing African agency must be considered within the context of how to enable an independent civil society that can withstand political and other pressures, but also be financially independent. While raising African philanthropic resources is certainly one option, more needs to be understood about how to enable civil society and philanthropic independence, particularly where civil society voices are threatened. These tasks may be huge, but they must be addressed.

References

Bomba, B. (2011) 'Zimbabwe Alliance, Seizing the Moment', *Alliance Magazine*, 16(1), pp. 41-43).

Extractive Industries Transparency Initiative (EITI) (2016) https://eiti.org/Liberia

Gladwell, M. (2000) *The Tipping Point: How Little Things Can Make a Big Difference*. Boston, Little, Brown.

Murisa, T. (2015) 'Not Yet Uhuru: Zimbabwe's Halting Attempts at Democracy', in T. Murisa and T. Chikweche (eds), *Beyond the Crises: Zimbabwe's Prospects for Transformation*. Dakar and Harare, TrustAfrica and Weaver Press.

Murisa, T. and T. Chikweche (eds), *Beyond the Crises: Zimbabwe's Prospects for Transformation*. Dakar and Harare, TrustAfrica and Weaver Press.

Murisa, T. and M. Nyaguse (2015) 'Arrested Development: An Analysis of Zimbabwe's Post-Independence Social Policy Regimes', in T. Murisa and T. Chikweche (eds), *Beyond the Crises: Zimbabwe's Prospects for Transformation*. Dakar and Harare, TrustAfrica and Weaver Press.

World Bank (2016) http://www.worldbank.org/en/country/zimbabwe/overview

5

Movement Building to Promote African Voices: TrustAfrica's support to stop illicit financial flows from Africa

Fambai Ngirande

Introduction

The topic of illicit financial flows (IFFs) may appear to be a specialised matter of concern only to technical experts, but TrustAfrica's project to curb IFFs from Africa demonstrates that it can be made the people's business. Over the past three years TrustAfrica and its partners have helped popularise the debate and build mass pressure to effect policy changes on what is now emerging as a critical development matter for the continent. This chapter unpacks the issue of IFFs and looks at the state of advocacy when TrustAfrica joined the space, the strategies employed, and the impact of the project's interventions.[1]

A conceptual look at illicit financial flows

The term 'illicit financial flows' has gained currency as a catch-all phrase that defines the leakage of resources across borders through a variety of hidden means. Global Financial Integrity (GFI) (2013) defines IFFs as 'all unrecorded private financial outflows involving capital that is il-

---

1   This chapter is based on a combination of documentary research and interviews with current and former TrustAfrica staff and funded partners of the IFF project.

legally earned, transferred, or utilised, generally used by residents to accumulate foreign assets in contravention of applicable capital controls and regulatory frameworks'. Thus, even if the funds are legitimate, such as the profits of a business, their transfer abroad in violation of exchange control regulations or corporate tax laws would render the capital illicit. The Organisation for Economic Cooperation and Development (2012), refers to IFFs as 'methods, practices and crimes aiming to transfer financial capital out of a country in contravention of national and international laws'. According to the United Nations Development Program (2011), IFFs 'include but are not limited to tax evasion, corruption, trade in contraband goods, and criminal activities such as drug trafficking and counterfeiting'. Varied as the definitions of IFFs are, implicit in all of them is the idea of concealing income or wealth from the relevant tax authorities.

The sources of IFFs fall into three broad categories: corporate, criminal and corrupt. The latter arise from activities such as the bribery of state officials and theft of state assets. Criminal sources are generated from money laundering, drug trafficking and human trafficking. Corporate sources derive from commercial activities of mostly private multinational companies and are estimated to account for 65% of all illicit outflows. As sensationalised as corruption is in narratives of the continent, the High Level Panel on Illicit Financial Flows from Africa (2013) estimated that corruption accounts for 5% of IFFs, with the remaining 30% coming from proceeds of crime.

Given its huge contribution to the overall volume of IFFs, the commercial component deserves particular attention. Companies employ a wide range of mechanisms to evade taxes and illicitly transfer funds from African countries, including transfer pricing, and misinvoicing trade and services. Multinational companies can engage in intra-group trade to move profits from high- to low-tax jurisdictions, and can also understate the quantity, price and quality of their exports, particularly in the extractive sector, resulting in losses in potential revenue for the exporting countries. As well, they may over-invoice imports in order to illegally export foreign currency, and invoice for fictitious agency fees, brand fees, and management fees.

Although the commercial sector is the biggest source of illicit financial flows from Africa, its role in undermining development on the continent is often overlooked. In fact, multinational companies are generally regarded as development saviours on the continent and foreign direct investment (FDI) is uncritically accepted as a panacea for the its development challenges. Development problems on the continent are usually attributed to the all-too-familiar problems of state corruption and bad governance. However, growing insights on IFFs demonstrates that the corporate sector, if not held accountable, can be an equally destructive force through IFFs, exacerbating the sector's culpability in Africa's underdevelopment. Indeed, corruption by state bureaucrats and IFFs perpetrated by corporate elites cannot be looked at in isolation. Often, there is collusion between the two, withering the capacities of African governments, corroding democratic institutions and compromising public officials. This in turn limits the state's capacity to dismantle the vicious cycle of exploitative conditions and unjust economic relations under which IFFs thrive. Even more worrisome for a war-weary continent is the fact that IFFs 'not only thrive in conflict and insecurity but exacerbate both by undermining the financial and political prospects for states to deliver and support development progress' (Cobham 2016).

The lack of transparency in the global financial architecture encourages IFFs. Tax havens and offshore jurisdictions facilitate layers of financial opacity and dubious accounting practices that create a shadow finance system in which IFFs thrive. In spite of its global spread, the most devastating effects of IFFs are felt in the developing world, Africa in particular; they constitute a major source of resource leakage from the continent, draining scarce foreign exchange reserves, reducing tax collection, counteracting investment inflows and ultimately contributing to worsening poverty and inequality. Reed and Fontana (2011) estimate that $1.3 trillion was illicitly siphoned out of the continent between 1980 and 2009. The report of the High Level Panel on IFFs from Africa estimates the annual leakages from the continent at up to $60 billion. The latest OECD estimates (2016) go as high as $150 billion per annum. Worse still, an influential GFI (2011) study estimated that illicit financial flows from Africa were increasing at an annual average of 23%.

Clearly, IFFs are a problem too big to ignore, not least by African countries whose development prospects depend on their ability to leverage their resources for development. In its groundbreaking advocacy campaign, 'Stop the Bleeding', TrustAfrica deliberately describes this leakage of Africa's wealth as a loss of blood, a metaphor that speaks to the life-threatening loss of domestic resources which could otherwise have been life-sustaining – if used to address healthcare, education, infrastructure, and other vital development priorities. This loss of resources not only retards development across the African continent but has corrosive impacts on governance and the enjoyment of human rights, the stability and security of societies, and the rule of law, democracy and justice.

Research carried out by the Mali-based Institute for Research and Policy Alternatives in Development (IRPAD) with support from TrustAfrica demonstrates that IFFs capitalise upon existing structural weaknesses in African countries (Goïta et al., 2015). These include inadequate legal frameworks; lack of enforcement of existing laws; poor contract negotiation and award processes; limited knowledge and awareness about IFFs and their manifestations; poor inter-country collaboration; lack of beneficiary ownership and disclosure, and poor coordination amongst stakeholders. The Swiss Agency for Development and Cooperation (2014) echoes these findings by noting that 'loop-holes in national legal systems, contradictions between them, and the capabilities gaps of developing countries to enforce them and international agreements, enable economic players and individuals to transfer financial resources internationally in a targeted way on a large scale'.

Exposing the rot: the emergence of a movement

Illicit financial flows are not a new phenomenon. In fact, the various schemes that add up to what is now conceptually defined as IFFs began with global capitalism. Yet for a long time, IFFs were largely perpetrated under the radar, with little literature and discussion on the subject. In the 1980s and 1990s, structural adjustment programs and the associated financial deregulation regimes that were introduced made possible the unhindered global mobility of capital, resulting in a massive increase in IFFs. It was not until recently, however, that IFFs aroused public attention. Baker (2005) provided empirical estimates on the extent of the problem at a global level, and Ndikumana and Boyce (2011) was amongst the pioneering works to provide Africa-specific context and estimates.

When TrustAfrica began work on IFFs in 2013, a number of international and African organisations were already working on the subject and related matters, including groups such as the UK-based Tax Justice Network (TJN), Oxfam, Action Aid and Tax Justice Network-Africa (TJN-A). Credit is due to all these groups, and in particular the efforts of African civil society, for putting issue at the forefront of development discussions on the continent.

TrustAfrica's decision to work on IFFs evolved from earlier initiatives supported with funds from the Ford Foundation. In the initial years after its founding in 2006, TrustAfrica utilised funding from the Ford Foundation and others for three broad programme areas: democratic governance, African philanthropy and equitable development. A few years ago, however, discussions between the Ford Foundation and TrustAfrica gravitated towards a narrower thematic focus, and IFFs emerged as the core issue supported with Ford Foundation funds. Commenting on this shift in focus, a then TrustAfrica programme staff member noted that the focus 'enabled us to connect themes in economic governance with elements of a much-needed developmental agenda centred on enhancing the African state's capacity to meet the needs of its people'. Around the same time there was also a growing interest across the continent in exploring domestic resource mobilisation as an alternative to external sources of finance that were proving to be inconsistent and unsustainable.

From the broad agreement to focus the funding on illicit financial flows, TrustAfrica proceeded to set its own goals, to outline strategies and to build a network of partners. When TrustAfrica entered the space, the conversation was dominated by voices in London, Brussels and Washington. The OECD analysis in particular dominated the discourse and shaped the thinking on policy responses. While this helped to bring to the fore the global aspects of IFFs, it did little to express or address the African specificities of the problem.

Given this context, TrustAfrica set its broad goal to support a movement promoting African voices in processes and initiatives that stop the flow of IFFs from the continent. It specifically outlined the following objectives:

1. Build and strengthen a wider movement of advocates rooted in Africa to combat illicit financial flows through the provision of platforms for dialogue, knowledge and experience sharing among advocacy, knowledge generation and policy formulation communities.

2. Expand and enhance access to needs-driven up-to-date research, data and analysis on the state, dynamics of economic governance and IFFs in Africa.

3. Communicate more effectively about illicit financial flows and ensure that there is a growing set of actors (experts and non-ex-

perts) in the debates and advocacy against illicit financial flows.

4. Foster networking, coordination and collaboration among institutions (including those in the global north) working on illicit financial outflows.

Underlying these objectives was TrustAfrica's overarching aim to facilitate the emergence of a critical mass of informed, networked, and resilient African civil society organisations capable of holding governments accountable to pro-poor policies. As TrustAfrica's IFF programme officer noted, 'we see our role as contributing to shifting the balance of power between self-interested elites and the people'. From TrustAfrica's perspective, work to put in place policies that stop IFFs is in many ways a political process that seeks changes in the distribution of wealth and power; getting to the tipping point requires the mobilisation of a robust movement to challenge entrenched interests and force reforms to the structures underpinning the global financial governance processes. To this end TrustAfrica's interventions have evolved into a cohesive programme of action whose main pillars go beyond grant-making to include research and knowledge management, capacity building and technical assistance, convening and campaigning.

Strengthening the African knowledge base

In order to feed the initiative's popular messaging and policy proposals, TrustAfrica and its partners invested in research on various aspects of IFFs. These efforts constitute a major part of TrustAfrica's goal to build a truly African advocacy movement to advance the issue. Research into IFFs is dominated by western institutions, in part because groups such as GFI and TJN have a much longer history of working on the issue and, more importantly, have access to the kind of resources needed to conduct in-depth research. Moreover, funding for such research is not easily available on the continent. As a result, African civil society actors have found themselves compelled to quote data and cite references from the West, which were not as helpful when it came to mobilising for local action.

Beyond the need for data, however, the larger perspective was at issue. As TrustAfrica's programme officer explained, 'we were acutely aware that we were joining a conversation that had been framed from an outside perspective and dominated by global north voices'. Thus the goal was not just to generate relevant research, but to propose solutions that would apply to the conditions on the continent. TrustAfrica's collaboration with the Accra-based Third World Network-Africa (TWN-A), which set out to unpack the conceptual and systemic aspects of the issue in Africa and put forward policy recommendations relevant to the 'African specificities', was a critical intervention in this regard. This 'conceptual clarification' identified the structural aspects of the challenge of IFFs to African economies. TrustAfrica then facilitated wider knowledge sharing to help strengthen the capacity of African civil society in general.

As part of an overall commitment to building a pan-African knowledge base, TrustAfrica has actively supported the strengthening of the capacities of African researchers on IFFs. It has afforded pan-African researchers the space and resources to tackle complex themes from an African perspective and, significantly, to contextualise some of the orthodox analysis that had in many cases inadequately captured the interests of African people. Over the last three years, TrustAfrica has brought together leading African scholars and researchers to explore ways of strengthening methodologies of studying IFFs. In addition, it has established an IFF Research Grants Initiative whose objective is to provide responsive and accessible technical and financial support for researchers. To date, research fellows from twelve African countries have accessed support from this facility and are contributing to the emergence of a cohesive body of knowledge influencing policy discussions and stimulating debate on IFFs.

This knowledge-building work has included studies on IFFs and the mining sector in five West African countries, namely Mauritania, Guinea, Burkina Faso, Niger and Mali. It also has included in-depth studies on the extent of IFFs in key economic sectors in Southern Africa, specifically focused on mining, agriculture, and wildlife and tourism. TrustAfrica has also been working with the Southern Africa Trust to build knowledge on the links between African philanthropy and illicit financial flows. From initial studies that looked at philanthropy's links to IFFs, natural resource governance and taxation, the Southern Africa Trust has brought the work to a regional level, with the Southern Africa Development Community (SADC) secretariat now exploring the development of a regional framework for sustainable financing for development which would have a major focus on curbing illicit financial flows. TrustAfrica has also collaborated with partners such as TJN-A to build knowledge on the issue of transfer pricing from an African perspective. The resulting policy recommendations on issues such as legislative reforms and regional approaches to taxation have strongly influenced positions advanced at regional and continental decision-making platforms.

Significantly, research by TrustAfrica and partners found that plugging IFF leakages and enhancing the extractive sector's contribution to public revenues and social development would have a greater developmental dividend across all five West African countries than FDI and Official Development Assistance (ODA) combined. While there is still a long way to go before African institutions can stand toe to toe with their Western counterparts in terms of research capacity and knowledge production, efforts by TrustAfrica and its partners show, at the very minimum, the importance of investing in local knowledge production to fuel the case for policy action.

In addition to commissioning original research, a signature TrustAfrica contribution has been the establishment of a free online database that serves as a 'knowledge hub' for IFFs from Africa. Established in partnership with the Southern Africa Research and Documentation Centre (SARDC), this database contains over 600 research papers, reports and other documents and keeps the community of researchers, civil society and policymakers updated on new resources via a system of alerts. Advocates view the growth of a database of credible data reflective of African perspectives as central to their ability to set the agenda and spearhead their own initiatives to combat IFFs.

Challenging dominant narratives

After entering the field at a time when the narrative on IFFs was largely dominated by organisations and platforms in the north, TrustAfrica has made a notable contribution by helping to amplify African voices on the issues. It has also helped build the capacity of African organisations to engage in policy conversations. Central to this has been TrustAfrica's investment in the reframing the debate to reflect African priorities and specificities. This new frame is expressed in 'The African CSOs IFF Declaration and Call to Action' developed by TrustAfrica and partners as part of the 'Stop the Bleeding' campaign.

One key area where TrustAfrica has differed with the international community has been the orthodox framing of IFFs. The dominant framing has been based on a minimalist focus on 'illegal' activities such as crime and corruption; it approaches the issue of IFFs in isolation and regards it as a new-found silver bullet to solve Africa's development problems. Challenging this framing, TrustAfrica has contributed to bringing attention to the structural weaknesses of the global economic governance system as the root cause of IFFs. It has further focused attention beyond 'illegal' activities to include 'legal' leakages of African resources that are taking place through, for instance, unregulated capital flight and tax holidays granted by African governments to multinational corporations. The new focus favoured by TrustAfrica has also helped strengthen the response of civil society in a way that reaches beyond the fixation on transparency and corruption that had come to define the Extractive Industry Transparency Initiative (EITI) responses. The EITI and even to an extent the Publish What You Pay (PWYP) based approach tends to let commercial companies off the hook and assumes that the problem is simply with African governments stealing monies paid by companies as tax revenues. TrustAfrica's contribution has therefore been to work with its partners to expand the spotlight and to also question whether companies are paying their fair share of taxation in the first place. The focus on corporate activities is sensible given the fact that the corporate sector is responsible for the bulk of IFFs. That this occurs as part of normal business practice is not as surprising as the fact that financial regulatory frameworks in African countries are largely unable to stem the resource leakages. This is compounded by the fact that the tepid global regulatory frameworks are rendered ineffectual by the lack of cooperation across borders.

Reflecting on Third World Network's (TWN) cooperation with TrustAfrica to expand the definition of IFFs to focus more on the root and structural causes, Yao Graham, TWN's coordinator, contends that 'anti-IFF interventions that carry the blessing of international financial institutions and major donors tend to focus around corruption, bribery and money laundering.' For example, the World Bank frequently refers to IFFs as comprising those flows and activities that have a clear connection with illegality. However, as research by TrustAfrica's partners consistently elaborates, the major source of resource leakages from Africa is not from the isolated behaviour of corrupt individuals in corporate entities but stems from unjust economic power relations between Africa and the developed world. IFFs have become a fundamental element of a business model favoured by transnational companies and enabled by a global economic governance architecture that prioritises corporate interests over citizens' rights. The structural viewpoint supported by TrustAfrica and its partners lends itself to a more expansive definition of IFFs that goes beyond crime, corruption and the illicit to also interrogate the equally damaging licit flows that have become standard corporate practice to reduce tax liability and the share of revenues that remain in host countries. This expanded definition enables advocates to advance a more comprehensive economic justice agenda and to interrogate the root and structural causes of gross resource leakages as part of a more holistic developmental and redistributive agenda, one that seeks to ensure that African populations in general – and not rich shareholders and politicians inside and outside the continent – become the biggest beneficiaries of the continent's resources.

Convening dialogues and connecting different actors

As most stakeholders working on IFFs would attest, a longstanding weakness of the African lobby on IFFs has been the absence of a coordinated voice. Given that the issue of IFFs from Africa is characteristically broad and composed of distinct country dynamics, arriving at a consensus was always bound to be a difficult undertaking. However, through convening and collaborative work, TrustAfrica has played a leading role in creating platforms that bring together civil society organisations for strategic consultations and for knowledge and experience sharing. As part of these efforts, TrustAfrica supported the formation of a Working Group on Illicit Financial Flows and Africa's Development. The working group brought together leading African organisations including the African Women's Development and Communication Network (FEMNET), the African Regional Organisation of the International Trade Union Confederation (ITUC-Africa), TJNA-A, the African Forum and Network on Debt and Development (AFRODAD), and TWN-A. It serves as a platform to strategise and operationalise coordinated responses. These efforts have contributed to a working convergence around the need to focus more on collective movement building and coordinated campaigns and advocacy instead of the tendency towards working in silos and remaining disconnected from grassroots constituencies.

Over the past three years TrustAfrica has organised, participated in and contributed to at least seven major convenings. These meetings brought together diverse stakeholders working on IFFs, including local communities, advocacy organisations, academics and policymakers. They ranged from high-level policy platforms such as the 'Pan African CSO Conference on Tax, DRM and IFF' to 'Building a People's Movement to curb IFF in Southern Africa' held as part of the Southern Africa People's Summit. The major thrust of these platforms has been for advocates to coordinate strategies, explore collaboration and facilitate the emergence of a coordinated African voice. The harmonisation of efforts has been instrumental not only in putting IFFs on the policy agenda in a more coherent way but also in enhancing African narratives as to how IFFs can be addressed. At the same time, the investment in convenings has enabled the emergence of a solid core of connected pan-African organisations with the technical capability and legitimacy to effectively shape and influence decision-making around IFFs.

Citizen mobilisation and policymaker engagement

Going beyond specialist policymaking platforms, TrustAfrica has also maintained fidelity to its commitment to broaden the movement of advocates on IFFs and bring the masses into the conversation. To this end, it has been working to weave elements of its interventions into a coordinated popular campaign, 'Stop the Bleeding'. With the target of mobilising one million signatures to demand action by African policymakers, TrustAfrica has partnered with a core group of civil society organisations across the continent to drive popular messages on IFFs and mobilise citizens to take action. The thinking behind the campaign is that policymakers will be compelled to act if citizens demonstrate that they care about this issue and unequivocally demand action from their leaders. The TrustAfrica approach is consistent with the findings of the High Level Panel on IFFs from Africa which concluded that 'political will is an essential ingredient' to policy change.

From the initial continental launch in Nairobi in June 2015, the campaign has been rolled out to West and Southern Africa sub-regions. In each sub-region a core group of partners is responsible for mobilising civil society and coordinating efforts to engage with policymakers at the national and regional economic community levels. Working with its partners TJN-A and TWN-A, TrustAfrica successfully made sure that IFFs featured prominently during the UN Third International Conference on Finance for Development (FFD3) in Addis Ababa in July 2015. As a result of these efforts, prominent figures, including former South African President Thabo Mbeki and United Nations Economic Commission for Africa Executive Secretary, Carlos Lopes, endorsed the campaign; it has also received support from Nobel Peace Prize Laureate Leymah Gbowee and UN Goodwill Ambassador, Yvonne Chaka Chaka, as well as from the global solidarity community, in particular groups such as the AFL-CIO's Solidarity Center, Jubilee USA and US-Africa Network.

Given their technical nature, raising popular awareness about IFFs has required advocates to adjust their messaging as they discover which aspects of the issue carry most popular appeal. The challenge is that it is remarkably difficult for ordinary people to establish the connection between multinational corporations, some of whom are the makers of beloved household brands, and the systematic bleeding of public resources. In response to this challenge, TrustAfrica has harnessed music, film, poetry, regalia and other forms of creative expression. In 2016, the campaign won, through a popular online vote, the Honesty Oscar for Best Activist Anthem. The stated aim of the Honesty Oscars Awards is to 'name and fame' those doing important work to bring about accountability. This is one indication that the campaign has effectively broken new ground in terms of reaching out into mass public consciousness beyond traditional organised civil society. The implications of this breakthrough is that the campaign can effectively be broadened through other mass mobilisation activities and bring grassroots voices to the forefront of IFFs advocacy.

Concurrent with citizen mobilisation, TrustAfrica has been investing in supporting civil society's direct engagements with policymakers. As a result of growing spotlight on IFFs, African leaders have been exploring various initiatives to respond to the problem. One such initiative is the High Level Panel on IFFs, which was established by African leaders motivated by the need to seek alternative sources of development financing to fulfil service delivery commitments in the context of declining economic growth and foreign direct assistance. This convergence of interests between African governments and independent actors in confronting IFFs might presuppose the emergence of improved state-civil society relations. On the contrary, TrustAfrica's experience has been that of progressive engagement with the African states at a continental level, and often fractious engagement at the national level. This is hardly surprising given the advocacy agenda of TrustAfrica and its partners which highlights the failure by African nations to shift from tax competition to tax cooperation; the complicity of some political elites in facilitating IFFs, particularly in the extractive sector; and the failure of African governments to agree on standard regulatory frameworks and accountability mechanisms for corporations in their jurisdictions. In spite of this challenging relationship with many nation states, TrustAfrica has continued to support initiatives to engage policymakers at the national level including legislators, revenue authorities and law enforcement agencies.

TrustAfrica has used platforms to engage with policymakers as opportunities to share research and policy recommendations coming from partners working on the ground. This kind of engagement has contributed to shifting the thinking of policymakers in many ways. In particular, African policymakers did not fully appreciate the need for a home-grown discourse on IFFs, thinking simply that the proposals that were coming from the OECD and Western governments would provide global solutions that would work for Africa as well. Now, there is an increased appreciation by policymakers of the need to nuance the 'African specificities' of IFFs and produce local data to guide action (UNECA, 2013). While getting policymakers to take decisive action is a daunting challenge, some traction is evident from TrustAfrica's efforts to support partner's participation in national forums and continental initiatives that provide important platforms to secure African policymakers' buy-in.

Whilst African actors have striven to rally behind their policymakers in efforts to combat IFFs, African policymakers have tended to display misplaced confidence in the global economic governance system's commitment to policing IFFs. This confidence has been incentivised somewhat by various initiatives on IFFs promoted by the World Bank, the IMF and the OECD. These organisations have over the years launched flagship initiatives on IFFs, mostly centred on tax rules and anti-corruption measures which in many ways represent a reaction to the extent to which the rules of international financial institutions are routinely subverted by IFFs. However, these initiatives characteristically do not go as far as questioning the asymmetrical power relations embedded in the rules that govern the global economic order. Whilst welcoming the important efforts of Western-dominated institutions to fight IFFs, TrustAfrica's chief concern is about the risks associated with outsourcing the resolution of Africa's developmental challenges to other actors. It is therefore not surprising to see across all of TrustAfrica's interventions the principle of African agency as the core driver of solutions to African problems.

Reflections on missed opportunities

Undoubtedly, TrustAfrica's efforts have 'shaped the game' through very positive influences in many respects. Perhaps most significant is its contribution to reframing the discourse on IFFs from an African perspective.

This has made the IFFs advocacy grounded, and relevant to African civil society and policymakers alike. Equally important, TrustAfrica's work has been instrumental in fostering collaboration among African institutions and in the process has contributed to the emergence of a coherent movement of African voices. However, there are also shortcomings, and missed opportunities. In particular, the project is in its third and final year of guaranteed funding without a clear plan of how the work will continue. TrustAfrica's partners on the ground whose projects are coming to an end are also not clear on where things will go from here. Perhaps TrustAfrica could have invested more in anticipating the end of guaranteed funding and worked more to build a diverse pool of funding beyond the initial funder. It appears as if from the onset TrustAfrica took a project support approach that meant mostly one-year agreements with partners – though this needs to be seen within the context of the yearly funding that TrustAfrica was receiving from its own donor. This short-term approach appears to have severely limited TrustAfrica's partners' ability to think more strategically beyond annual project timeframes. Further, the short-term thinking seems to have limited TrustAfrica's contribution to core support and sustainability of institutions working on IFFs.

In some instances, mostly due to limited funding, TrustAfrica has had to move away from projects at the end of the one-year project implementation period, even if they were clearly successful. This contradiction between a commitment to building and sustaining a long-term movement on IFFs and the reality of short-term project modalities limits continuity and connectedness of interventions. Moving into the future, TrustAfrica may want to consider working with partners on a minimum three-year cycle and to stay with successful partners.

Conclusion

As the first three-year cycle of TrustAfrica's work on IFFs draws to an end its legacy is a growing movement of trained people and a credible body of knowledge making the case that IFFs are one of the most pernicious development challenges confronting the Africa today and that stopping them requires the concerted efforts of a movement of empowered actors from the continent. TrustAfrica's role in catalysing the emergence of such a movement and popularising the issue of IFFs in three years is a phenomenal achievement and a strong basis to build upon future endeavours in pursuit of a more just and accountable global economic governance system. The body of work under review demonstrates with remarkable clarity not only the impact, but also the resourcefulness of African institutional responses to problems affecting the continent. Specifically, interventions that are rooted in an understanding of the specificities of Africa's challenges can strike at the root and structural causes. This points to the difference that can be made by a philanthropic organisation that is based on the continent and focused on African agency. It is demonstrated by the wholly original conceptualisation of TrustAfrica's IFF interventions that put people's lives at the centre of analysis, research, and subsequent action. In so doing, it has galvanised a new constituency – and helped organisations to coalesce around a movement whose growing influence has made important inroads in undermining the pervasively negative impacts of IFF on the African continent.

References

Baker, R. (2005) *Capitalism's Achilles' Heel: Dirty money and how to renew the free market system.* London, John Wiley and Sons.

Baker, R. (2013) *IFF from Developing Countries: Measuring OECD Responses IFFs from Africa: A hidden resource for Development*, available on www.gfintegrity.org

Ndikumana, L. and J.K. Boyce (2011) *Africa's Odious Debts: How Foreign Loans and Capital Flight Bled a Continent*, London, Zed Books.

Cobham, A. (2016) 'Breaking the vicious circles of illicit financial flows, conflict and insecurity', *Great Insights Magazine*, 5(1).

United Nations Economic Commission for Africa (UNECA) (2013) 'Illicit Financial Flows: Report of the High Level Panel on Illicit Financial Flows from Africa'. Addis Ababa, UNECA.

Global Financial Integrity (2013) *IFFs from Africa: A hidden resource for development,* available on www.gfintegrity.org

Goïta, M. et al. (2015) 'Synthetic report of five studies on Illicit Financial Flows (Burkina Faso, Guinea, Mali, Mauritania and Niger)'. Bamako, IRPAD.

Organisation for Economic Co-operation and Development (OECD) (2014) 'Illicit financial flows from developing countries: Measuring OECD Responses'. Paris, OECD.

Ritter, I. (2011) *Illicit Financial Flows: An Analysis and some Initial Policy*

Proposals, Frankfurt, Friedrich-Ebert-Stiftung.

UNDP (2011) *Illicit Financial Flows from Least Developed Countries 1990 – 2008*, New York, UNDP, available on http://www.undp.org/content/undp/en/home/librarypage/povertyreduction/trade_content/illicit_financialflowsfromtheleastdevelopedcountries1990-2008.html

6

Opening up the Policy Process: TrustAfrica's work to include the voices of smallholder farmers

Chipo Plaxedes Mubaya

Introduction

In Africa, the only region in the world where poverty and hunger are on the rise, agriculture remains critical for poverty reduction. Yet the continent's agricultural productivity is on the decline, and in some cases has stagnated (ADB, 2012; Practical Action and PELUM, 2005). This situation is compounded by a multiplicity of challenges, including limited access to agricultural inputs, water, markets and knowledge as well by the effect of climate change (Boko et al., 2007; Mano and Nhemachena, 2008). For these reasons, aid and investment remain important, yet European Commission aid to African agriculture is declining. Furthermore, existing aid and investment tends to undermine poor farmers, who constitute 60% of African smallholder farmers (Practical Action and PELUM, 2005). This is a cause for concern, given that more than two-thirds of the population in Sub-Saharan Africa is based in rural areas, and of those, 70% depend on crop and livestock farming for their livelihood (ibid.).

In this context, implementing policies to increase smallholder agricultural productivity is a strategy that promises to achieve pro-poor growth (Birner, 2010). This will require macroeconomic policies such as removing the agricultural taxes that threaten African farmers, improving services and investments in agricultural technology, and boosting agricultural performance through the engagement of farmers' networks and organisations (Binswanger-Mkhize and McCalla, 2010). The continent's leaders have voiced their support for smallholder support, but with rare exceptions they have failed to make the necessary investments. Progress on this front requires concerted action to improve the ability of farmers' networks and civil society organisations to influence policymaking.

Since 2009, TrustAfrica has leveraged donor funds in order to build an effective advocacy movement for smallholder agriculture, and to increase farmer participation in decision making regarding agricultural policies on the continent. This chapter seeks to explore the impact of that work. It frames the discussion in terms of African agency, and reflects on whether it has made a difference to have an African-led, Africa-based philanthropy operating in this space. The chapter was informed by academic research, a review of grant documentation, and interviews with TrustAfrica's funded partners, donors and staff.

Agency in agriculture

The literature on agency highlights the duality of structure: that the agent both shapes, and is shaped by, the structure in which it exists (Chambers, 1989; Giddens, 1984, 1991, 1994, 2009). Moreover, group actions constitute an important element of processes of social cohesion and innovation in responding to environmental, social, economic and political threats (Mutopo, 2014). This contrasts with dominant and normative thinking of the poor as hopeless, a construction that is consistent with dependence on donors and other external agencies at the expense of people's own agency (Kithiia, 2010).

Alternative literature highlights the need to understand agency in the context of agriculture in Africa – in which farmers are highlighted as innovators, and technical and socio-cultural creators – as opposed to approaches that rarely take into account the ability of farmers to respond to shocks that threaten agricultural productivity (Crane et al., 2011). In this context, agency in agriculture is best understood in the realm of 'agriculture as performance', which recognises farmers' creative capacities to respond to socioeconomic and environmental challenges – that they react to challenges and opportunities as they arise in agriculture systems (Richards, 1989, 1993).

This literature on 'agriculture as performance' views agricultural knowledge as something that is held with some degree of spontaneity, as opposed to an intellectual expertise that is employed to reach a decision. Agency in agriculture is thus best understood as farmers' actions transcending specific planned technical behaviours on farms to performing roles as members of social networks and collectivities (Crane et al., 2011). TrustAfrica's work in smallholder agriculture builds on this understanding by focusing on building the capacity of smallholder farmers, their associations and unions, and civil society formations to advocate for improved policies and locally owned and led agricultural development agendas.

TrustAfrica's work in agricultural advocacy

TrustAfrica serves as an intermediary, a Southern-based organisation that provides funding to other African organisations, a role hitherto largely played by Northern institutions. Even as it disburses funds that originate in the global north, its presence on the continent results in a different way of operating, according to organisation staff and partners. TrustAfrica's philanthropic work recognises the importance of agency and is based on the premise that equitable and sustainable agricultural development is possible through concerted advocacy by African stakeholders. This approach tends to align itself with alternative forms of operations that empower local level structures and institutions to play a greater role in self-mobilisation processes (Mubaya et al., 2015).

TrustAfrica took into account a number factors when initiating its agriculture policy advocacy work. These include the importance of building skilled, networked, and active agricultural advocacy organisations across the continent; the need for credible and inclusive platforms and forums to foster transparent and productive policy dialogues amongst all stakeholders; and the imperative to pilot innovative strategies in selected countries that present learning and replication opportunities. Ultimately, TrustAfrica aimed to create a vibrant agriculture advocacy movement.

The context in Sub-Saharan Africa

Current policymaking processes on the continent limit the meaningful engagement of civil society and smallholder voices, including limited conceptualisation and recognition of policymaking spaces and limited opportunities to engage these voices (Bank, 2011; Kithiia, 2010). Local governments and farmer organisations have not been adequately empowered through fiscal decentralisation and community-driven development. Dr. Lindiwe Majele-Sibanda, a leading farmer advocate and CEO of FANRPAN,[1] observes that although Africa has an oral culture, Africans do not talk enough when and where it matters most – at the local, national and regional levels. Rather, the dialogue happens more at the international level, where the few speak for the majority (Majele-Sibanda, 2013).

TrustAfrica saw an opportunity to make a difference in this regard. In July 2003 all 53 African governments at the African Union summit in Maputo agreed to make agriculture a top priority in national development, signing on to the Comprehensive Africa Agriculture Development Programme (CAADP). Parties to the agreement made a commitment to 'increase public investment in agriculture by a minimum of 10% of their national budgets' and to 'improve the productivity of agriculture to attain an average annual growth rate of 6%, with particular attention to smallholder farmers, especially focusing on women,' by the year 2015 (NEPAD, 2003).

But in the years since 2003, little had been done and few leaders had lived up to the rhetoric. In this context, TrustAfrica recognised the importance of agency to improving agricultural performance in Africa. Indeed, a review of CAADP's first phase noted challenges that lend weight to the TrustAfrica drive: a lack of clarity about the roles and responsibilities of different stakeholders; difficulties with the integration of gender-related issues and indicators into the plan; and inadequate coordination structures at all levels.

Elements of TrustAfrica's agriculture advocacy work

In 2009, TrustAfrica launched a programme in partnership with the Bill and Melinda Gates Foundation with the stated aim of building a more effective advocacy movement for sustainable agriculture in Africa. This programme recognises the importance of agency in agriculture and farming organisations in Africa by strengthening policy advocacy capacities within smallholder farmers' unions, associations and intermediary NGOs. TrustAfrica implemented this program in three sub-regions of Africa: West (Ghana and Nigeria), East (Tanzania, Uganda and Kenya) and South (Malawi). In 2013, TrustAfrica initiated the second phase of the project, 'Advocacy for Smallholder Farmers', in which it seeks to re-

---

1   FANRPAN, the Food Agriculture and Natural Resources Policy Analysis Network, is a pan-African organisation based in Pretoria, South Africa.

solve the uneven participation that has characterised policy reform processes and to ensure that chosen policy and strategy interventions are acceptable to the smallholder community and sustainable within mutual accountability (a key aspect of the second CAADP phase). A key aim was to build an African movement for policy advocacy and to raise awareness about the CAADP. While in the first phase TrustAfrica focused on one of the four CAADP major pillars[2] – food supply and hunger alleviation – staff broadened their focus in the second phase to include the issue of markets. TrustAfrica settled on these pillars mainly as a strategic imperative but also because its funding could only address so much.

TrustAfrica initialised the first phase of the project through a systematic scoping study to identify civil society organisations in Africa that are engaged in agriculture policy advocacy.[3] During the course of the project they hosted a series of convenings for all funded partners. One of these, in Lilongwe, aimed to help build the capacity of partners to participate in the formulation and implementation of agricultural policies, particularly within the CAADP framework. It also helped to familiarise partners with agricultural policies, networking and budget processes. TrustAfrica funds and activities sought to mobilise local-level participation in policy processes, and improve advocacy capacities for the budgeting and extension work.[4]

Outcomes and achievements of the work

Awareness raising and policy advocacy within the
CAADP framework

A key achievement at the start of the programme was the identification and engagement of civil society and farmer organisations, some of which

---

2   The four pillars focus on land and water management, market access, food supply and hunger alleviation and agricultural research.

3   The country scoping studies were published in a volume entitled 'From Rhetoric to Policy Action: An Analysis of Agricultural Policy Reform in Six African Countries' (available at www. trustafrica.org).

4   For instance, a range of these projects focused on sensitizing and educating farmers on CAADP (SEND Ghana, ECASARD, Farmers Union of Malawi, NASFAM, Centre for Land Economy and Rights of Women (CLEAR)), building capacity and understanding in budgeting processes and engaging local governments in the process (Peasant Farmers Association of Ghana (PFAG), NASFAM), extension (Farmers Union of Malawi) and communicating policy processes through the media (Jamaa Resources Initiative, Resource Conflict Institute for Land and Environment (RECONCILE), PFAG).

were rarely visible on the national scene but which had some potential to engage in policy advocacy. Importantly, the targeted organisations directly represent smallholder farmers' interests, engaging with farmers on the ground as opposed to reaching them indirectly through other organisations. One such organisation in Malawi, for instance, has more than 110,000 members across the country and is owned by farmers themselves. The role of this organisation is to encourage smallholder farmers to approach farming as a business and to conduct activities in groups. Many of the selected organisations had policy advocacy as a primary mandate (for some, research also formed part of their core work) making it easier to build in additional policy advocacy components as opposed to having to introduce the concept. TrustAfrica staff believe that these factors make it more likely that the work will not only be sustained but expanded as association members bring their knowledge of CAADP processes and principles and their policy advocacy skills to other groups with which they are affiliated. For the most part, partner organisations had not heard of CAADP before, despite the fact that as smallholder organisations they were the ultimate beneficiaries of its activities. CAADP now has better visibility and has been popularised at lower levels in the project districts and countries.

Reflections from funded partners indicate that this not only helped enlighten these partners on CAADP processes and principles, but did so in a way that ensured that the individuals and organisations involved became aware of the importance of advocacy. Furthermore, interviews with partners show that the widening of their knowledge base, when combined with enriched core activities and improved project ideas, led them to engage in policy advocacy in relation to CAADP.

Enhancing organisational capacity

As discussed above, partner organisations found the training offered to be appropriate and timely, and their enhanced capacity can be seen in their contributions to a number of policy initiatives undertaken in the various project countries. It can also be seen in the increased visibility enjoyed by some of the organisations that were previously little known. It helped that TrustAfrica deliberately chose partner organisations which, with a few exceptions, had the capacity to engage with large numbers of smallholder farmers. This ensured widespread participation in important agriculture-related activities, resulting in higher visibility and potentially contributing to long-lasting impact at the national level.

An example was a partner in Malawi that was able to successfully engage farmers to identify challenges related to agricultural policy advocacy and later take up the priority challenges in a high-level workshop. In Ghana, respondents noted that no organisation had hitherto succeeded in bringing farmers directly into the agriculture policy spaces, reflecting the value of TrustAfrica's support in enabling new voices to enter the policy discourse. Interviews further revealed that partners have managed to garner further support to carry forward agriculture policy work with farmers.

Building an effective advocacy movement for smallholder agriculture

Further evidence of partners' enhanced capacity can be seen in the increasing number of farmers who took part in negotiations and engagement with higher-level institutions involved in agriculture policymaking. As momentum began to build, and groups saw the need to work together and also collaborate with policymakers, a loose movement began to take hold. Examples include Ghana, where three partners were working and reports describe how engaged farmers have developed the confidence to request information from the district officials regarding the budget process and other issues. They also report improved collaboration between the district director of the Ministry of Food and Agriculture (MoFA) and farmers within the district. Projects centred on intensifying agriculture extension services and training farmers in their districts. In the same context, two partners highlighted that local level advocacy groups among farmers and NGOs were created and nurtured through the second phase of the project, where farmers were able to give input into the 2016 national budget, which reflected a 17.8% increase over the 2015 budget. Also in Ghana, one of the three partners indicated that they established a powerful Women Agriculture Advocacy Team that has managed to engage government through district structures, with farmers making presentations to policymakers. In this seemingly small but ultimately significant way, TrustAfrica initiated the process of bringing farmers to collaborate with relevant national policymaking teams.

At the end of the day, perhaps the most gratifying factor in any planned intervention is the ability to sustain activities beyond the funded intervention. Reflections from partners indicate that the Women Agriculture Advocacy Team and farmers' group have been involved in other activities beyond the TrustAfrica-funded project activities and the same groups were brought on board in the second phase of the project. These reflections resonate with those coming from Malawi and Uganda, where the training of trainers has created a pool of community trainers on agriculture policy related issues. Building local capacity in this way enables training to be done on an ongoing basis by fellow farmers rather than relying on external funding.

Collaboration

TrustAfrica's efforts illuminate the potential to build and sustain national movements through organisation-based collaboration. In Ghana and Malawi, there is evidence that collaboration was beginning to foster such movements at the national level. Two organisations in Ghana collaborated at the end of the first phase to prepare a joint project proposal for the second phase, which was eventually funded. Partners in Ghana and Malawi advanced collaboration in their projects by participating in each other's activities, for example through workshops that the collaborating organisations co-hosted under the TrustAfrica-funded projects. Clearly, TrustAfrica did catalyse collaboration among smallholder farmer organisations and can further facilitate this process to enhance sustainability.

Challenges and lessons learnt

While TrustAfrica's approach towards policy advocacy has started to register success in terms of enhancing national movements for agricultural policy advocacy, the processes have not been smooth. Several challenges have been noted by TrustAfrica staff and its partners, some of them consistent with documented challenges to policy advocacy across Africa. Some of the gaps faced in the first phase are currently being addressed in the second phase of the project.

Insufficient and short-term resources

Limited funding and resources regularly threaten the success of project implementation in agriculture policy advocacy (Schönfeldt and Hall, 2013). In this case, partners lamented the limited logistical support for agriculture budget tracking and advocacy activities. While there have been significant efforts to link farmers with the national budget and policymaking processes, there has been little support for farmers' follow-up activities with government after the budget and policy documents have been finalised. The critical point is the farmers' ability and capacity to track policy and determine the extent to which they are contributing to the policy processes. Partners highlighted that from their experience in implementing projects, advocacy activities may require funding for two or three years. Any funders considering implementing similar work need to take into account the need for an improved funding base and extended project period that has the potential to result in meaningful impact and, ultimately, transformation. Examples given by partners include limited capacity to conduct more local-level activities on the ground with farmers as well as the national level activities that TrustAfrica funded.

TrustAfrica and other philanthropic organisations may thus need to reconsider the amount and period of funding that they extend to their partners in order to address the challenge of limited capacity to follow through initiated activities. However, within this context, it is important to consider the funding dynamics for TrustAfrica, which is in reality both a funded and funding institution. This factor has implications for the nature and extent of directed resources and subsequently sustainability and continued funding for partners; it implicitly calls for long-term collaborations with other funding organisations to enable wider coverage and further depth of funding. In addition, TrustAfrica may need to consider other options such as diversifying its funding sources, building a stronger endowment fund, and funding partnerships with public and private financing. TrustAfrica and other funding organisations may also need to consider facilitating more effective local level community resource mobilisation for development.

Weak stakeholder engagement and relations

State and non-state actors are often in competition with each other when they operate within the same advocacy spaces. This competition can degenerate into conflict, especially with the increasing role of non-state players such as the private sector. TrustAfrica may have occasionally failed to anticipate and prepare for this challenge. This is important given reports of suspicion between civil society organisations (CSOs) and government institutions, which limited the extent to which civil society could engage in public policymaking, along with weak institutions and inadequate platforms for such engagement. Ideally, the roles of these two stakeholders are complementary, in that while CSOs can make policy more relevant, the government is better placed to serve farmers. TrustAfrica may need to consider investing in building relations between state and non-state actors in addition to building farmer capacity. Within this context, there is merit in understanding the role of the media in balancing smallholder farmer interests against political interests. For example, one organisation in Ghana made extensive use of the press to highlight farmer activities.

In Uganda and Kenya, reports indicated limited engagement of farmers with government due to factors at project, organisational and national levels. These included poor organisation by partners, bureaucracy, and fragile political situations. In other instances limited organisational integration of the projects beyond individual staff members led to a loss of project memory due to high staff turnover. Other disturbances were due to changes of governments. TrustAfrica and other funders may need to consider the potential for such changes to affect project implementation and stability.

High partner expectations

The complexities involved in multiple contracts and partnerships come with challenges that TrustAfrica and other funders must take into account. One of these is stakeholder perception management, as when partners' high financial expectations were accompanied by what some perceived as limited transparency regarding TrustAfrica's funding plans and capacity. It appears that TrustAfrica may not have adequately spelled out the extent of its support to partners. Communication with partners is therefore critical at an early stage. It may help to make clear that project funds are not intended to cover the organisations' administrative costs. On the other hand, some partners need such assistance, and including a budget line for it could make a difference in terms of increasing their capacity to manage and implement projects. Another way TrustAfrica and other funders can circumvent this challenge is to engage partners at an early stage in the design of their projects.

In addition, donors should complement traditional funding sources with more innovative approaches revolving around community resource mobilisation. In particular, youth and women are key, as they are at the centre of agricultural activities and may constitute powerful pressure groups for this process. In this context, conducting power analyses and making use of champions from farmer groups has the potential to advance agriculture policymaking. Funders may then be able to deal with stakeholder perception management more easily through a shared responsibility and local empowerment to promote community responsibility for the project. In addition to dealing with high stakeholder perceptions, this has the potential to limit the subordination of communities to external agencies.

Limited baseline engagements and assessments

While TrustAfrica does not play an agenda-setting role for partners, it certainly should play a role of encouraging evidenced-based project design. The research component that is usually important as a precursor to agriculture policy advocacy may have been given limited attention in the funded projects. There were reports that while TrustAfrica itself did a wide scoping study (mentioned earlier) it did little to encourage and sensitise its partners to the importance of conducting baseline rapid assessments of targeted smallholder farmers at the beginning of projects in order to understand farmers' priorities for advocacy. One way that TrustAfrica and other funders can ensure that this happens is to make baseline studies a pre-condition for grant awards at the proposal stage, since some of the partners did not see the need for this assessment.

It should be noted that one of the partners in Ghana and another one in Uganda did conduct baseline assessments as a precursor to the implementation of their projects. In Uganda, this included a participatory baseline stakeholder engagement process to understand seed varieties and appropriate agronomic practices with the assistance of research institutions, thus enabling more targeted activities. One of the partners in Malawi highlighted that 'good advocacy is normally that which is evidence and priority based', but said that limited funding did not allow for this process. TrustAfrica could consider creating incentives for partners to initiate farmer engagement activities with no financial support. This can be done through the provision of non-financial incentives. For example, TrustAfrica could award grants to those partners who show evidence of initiating community engagements and baseline studies into existing projects. Another way of promoting alternative resource mobilisation strategies is by encouraging partners to leverage existing grants with other, new, partners, as was done by one of the organisations in Ghana.

Limited focus on women and gender

While a few partners had a deliberate focus on gender and women, most did not. This focus is important given the central role that women and youth play and can play in increasing agricultural productivity. Women are employed in the agriculture sector and produce nearly 90% of the food on the continent (FAO 2012) yet they have little voice in the development of agricultural policies. It is thus critical for TrustAfrica and other funders to empower small organisations that deal directly with smallholder farmers in terms of human resources management and institutional strengthening (Daugbjerg and Swinbank, 2012; Schönfeldt and Hall, 2013). Women also carry a disproportionate burden of looking after and feeding the family. Meanwhile, youth constitute a significant percentage of the population in Africa and face high levels of unemployment (FAO, 2016).

In the current phase of this work, TrustAfrica has funded projects with a significant focus on women-specific movements for policy advocacy and equitable resources and markets, for instance in Burkina Faso. But since this work has only recently been initiated, it may be premature to focus on any achievements and challenges at this point. In Ghana, the project focuses on strengthening smallholder – and particularly women's – capacity and role in budget advocacy and monitoring increases in public investment for the targeted delivery of extension services.

Towards an effective framework for agriculture policy advocacy

In order to sustain its work to support advocacy campaigns and make a significant impact on agriculture policy in Africa, TrustAfrica may consider the following strategies and options.

Engagement of the media to help advance visibility

While it is important to connect farmers with government and other CSOs and NGOs working in agriculture, it remains critical to create awareness and to disseminate intervention-related information to the general public, farmer organisations and other development partners. To this end, TrustAfrica and other funders could support their partners to develop an advocacy, media and communication strategy either individually or in collaboration. Media engagement forms part of the advocacy campaign as their representatives have the potential to participate in agriculture advocacy fora. Traditional media, website and multi-media have the potential to raise the profile of farmers' activities and impact. For agriculture advocacy to remain relevant, it is important to focus on dynamic forms of media engagement, among them social media and other new platforms that capture the interest of socio-economic groups such as the youth, who also potentially have a role to play in agriculture advocacy.

Transnational collaboration on advocacy

For TrustAfrica and other philanthropic organisations to achieve the goal of building continental movements of policy advocacy, it is important to consider deliberate efforts to engage in transnational advocacy activities. These partnerships may work in collaboration to challenge state control of information and making use of technology to empower transnational advocacy through the efforts of new actors, among them smallholder farmers. Negotiating for policy change is an activity that requires coalitions of actors at various levels and with substantial mobilisation of resources for the strategic actions that direct outcomes of the process (Marfo and Mckeown, 2013). As opposed to international relations, transnational advocacy is advanced by non-state actors and can have a profound effect on domestic policy. TrustAfrica has stated its interest in contributing to the process of building a continental movement by facilitating, where appropriate, a unified voice for its partners and the organisations and farmers they represent.

TrustAfrica will need to analyse and understand the range of participation and accountability that a transnational campaign can pursue for optimum continental policy advocacy, and will need to take into account the difficulties of transnational advocacy, among them the geographical and culture distance between players (Meierotto, 2009) and the dynamics of the potentially problematic relationships among transnational NGOs and their networks (Jordan and van Tuijl, 2000).

Enhanced focus on direct smallholder participation

Reflections on the current efforts by TrustAfrica and others documented in literature (Meierotto, 2009) agree that there may be inherent challenges to local inclusion and participation in policy advocacy, particularly if the locals are not involved right at the beginning of the process. TrustAfrica may need to further enhance its focus on direct smallholder representation and participation as a way of advancing people-centred regional integration on agriculture policy in a framework where parliaments and non-state actors are all taken on board in shaping the continental agenda. The literature recommends baseline assessments that account for different value systems and perceptions of reality, including smallholder farmer prioritisation of issues and decision making within heterogeneous contexts (Poole and Msoni, 2013). The premise is that one must understand the context as seen by those people who experience it, and explore the constraints and strategies to deal with them at an early stage, as this is likely to result in more relevant and sustained outputs and outcomes (Forrester et al., 2008).

Conclusions

TrustAfrica's theory of change is centred on leveraging resources and ideas and building movements to advance equitable development and democracy in Africa. In its work in the agriculture sector, TrustAfrica has engaged with national smallholder farmer organisations to facilitate farmer agency in a unique way. This strategy is unique; in the past, it is larger CSOs that have engaged government on pro-poor policies that address smallholder farmer challenges.

This chapter has provided the context for TrustAfrica's efforts and highlights the traditional dichotomy between policy advocates and farmers. Policy advocates have been at the forefront of the policymaking process, largely without active involvement of the farmer on the ground. In contrast, TrustAfrica has created a platform that supports farmers' agency, engaging smallholder farmer organisations that are themselves made up of farmer organisations and representatives.

It is worth noting that this Africa-led and Africa-based philanthropy has given space for African smallholder agency at the lowest level, as opposed to conventional approaches that attempts to reach farmers through higher level intermediaries. TrustAfrica recognised that sustainable and equitable development policies are largely the result of a combination of advocacy efforts between grassroots-based actors (movements), intermediary NGOs and policy research institutions. However, the least influential stakeholders in the agricultural field are poor small-scale farmers, the majority of whom are rural women. Their lack of influence is a major obstacle to equitable and sustainable agricultural development in Africa.

Despite efforts to engage and empower government and farmer organisations, a scan of the policy advocacy landscape in Africa indicates that a lot more effort still needs to be made. This includes the transformation of the architecture of advocacy-oriented organisations to strengthen the participation of civil society in regional policy dialogue. For instance, the Southern Africa Trust is working on the development of structured mechanisms to enable civil society voices to be heard in regional policy processes. Equally important are strategic efforts by FANRPAN to place policy research at the forefront of the regional agenda, along with capacity building, institutional collaboration, resource mobilisation and information and communication management. While TrustAfrica has in the past engaged in similar efforts through its broader governance work, it has much to learn in applying such efforts to its specific work on agriculture policy advocacy. These complementary efforts can go a long way towards ensuring that the voices of the poor are heard in the agriculture policy formation arenas.

Elsewhere in the region, in Zambia, the creation of a multi-stakeholder platform the Agriculture Consultative Forum (ACF), made up of government players, civil society, farmers and the private sector, significantly shaped the way the agricultural sector has been run in the country since 2003. Among the achievements of the ACF are the facilitation of stakeholder input into the development of the Zambia CAADP Compact, which was later signed in 2011, and the support for the development of the agriculture chapter of the 5th and 6th National Development Plans. This provides a potential model for transformation in other African countries. While TrustAfrica intervention countries can learn from this the importance of developing multi-stakeholder platforms, the Zambian ACF can learn from the TrustAfrica model by more significantly engaging smallholder farmers, who form the bulk of the farmers in the country.

This chapter has presented evidence to the effect that TrustAfrica's approach has made considerable strides in bringing the farmer closer to the policymaking process. This approach subscribes to the agency and 'agriculture as performance' thesis put across at the beginning of the chapter, in which farmers have, unlike before, been afforded an opportunity to contribute to national budgeting and decision-making processes. TrustAfrica has also engaged marginalised socio-economic groups, particularly women, through partner organisations. However, TrustAfrica's approach would be more complete with further engagement of the youth who have potential for providing both real stability and positive transformation. In essence, African philanthropy that is committed to African agency must put even more emphasis on being inclusive to ensure that its efforts reach the local-level marginalised groups in society.

References

Bank, L. (2011) *Home Spaces, Street Styles: Contesting Power and Identity in a South African City*. London, Pluto Press.

Birner, R. (2010) 'The Political Economy of Policies for Smallholder Agriculture', *World Development*, Vol. 38, Issue 10, pp. 1442-1452.

Binswanger-Mkhize, H. and A.F. McCalla (2010) 'The Changing Context and Prospects for Agricultural and Rural Development in Africa', *Handbook of Agricultural Economics*, 4, pp. 3571-3712.

Boko, M., I. Niang, A. Nyong, C. Vogel, A. Githeko, M. Medany, B. Osman-Elasha, R. Tabo and P. Yanda (2007) 'Africa Climate Change 2007: Impacts, Adaptation and Vulnerability', in M.L. Parry, O.F. Canziani, J.P. Palutikof, P.J. van der Linden and C.E. Hanson (eds), *Contribution of Working Group II to the Fourth Assessment Report of the Intergovernmental Panel on Climate Change*. Cambridge, Cambridge University Press.

Chambers, R. (1989) 'Vulnerability: How the poor cope', *IDS Bulletin*, 20(2), pp. 33-40.

Crane, T.A., C. Roncoli and G. Hoogenboom (2011) 'Adaptation to climate change and climate variability: The importance of understanding agriculture as performance', *NJAS-Wageningen Journal of Life Sciences*, 57(3-4), pp. 179-185.

Daugbjerg, C., and A. Swinbank (2012) 'An introduction to the "new" politics of agriculture and food', *Policy and Society*, 31(4), pp. 259-270.

FAO (2016) 'Why Gender.' Rome, FAO. Accessed on 10 January 2016 from http://www.fao.org/gender/gender-home/gender-why/why-gender/en/

Forrester, J., A.G. Swartling and K. Lonsdale (2008) 'Stakeholder engagement and the work of SEI: An empirical study'. Stockholm, Stockholm Environment Institute.

Giddens, A. (1984) *The Constitution of Society*. Berkeley, CA, University of California Press.

Giddens, A. (1991) *The Consequences of Modernity*. Cambridge, Polity Press.

Giddens, A. (1994) 'Living in a Post-Traditional Society', in U. Beck, A. Giddens and S. Lasch, *Reflexive Modernization: Politics, Tradition and Aesthetics in the Modern Social Order*. Cambridge, Polity Press.

Giddens, A. (2009) *Sociology*. Polity Press.

Jordan, L. and P. van Tuijl (2000) 'Political Responsibility in Transnational NGO Advocacy', *World*

Kithiia J. (2010) 'Old notion-new relevance: setting the stage for the use of social capital resource in adapting East African coastal cities to climate change', *International Journal of Urban Sustainable Development*, 1, pp. 17-32.

Majele-Sibanda, L (2013) 'A Social Innovation to Solve the African Food and Nutrition Paradox'. Presentation to the Global Food Security Symposium, Washington, DC, 21 May.

Mano, R. and C. Nhemachena (2008) 'Assessment of the economic impacts of climate change on agriculture in Zimbabwe: a Ricardian approach'. CEEPA Discussion Paper No. 11. Centre for Environmental Economics and Policy in Africa. Pretoria, University of Pretoria.

Marfo, E. and J.P. Mckeown (2013) 'Negotiating the supply of legal timber to the domestic market in Ghana: Explaining policy change intent using the Advocacy Coalition Framework', *Forest Policy and Economics*, 32, pp. 23–31.

Meierotto, L. (2009) 'The uneven geographies of transnational advocacy: The case of the Talo Dam', *Journal of Environmental Management,* 90(3), pp. S279–S285.

Mubaya, C.P., P. Mutopo and R. Ndebele-Murisa (2015) 'Local level opportunities to deal with climate risk and vulnerability in Dar es Salaam', in A. Allen, A. Lampis and M. Swilling (eds) *Untamed Urbanisms*. New York, Routledge

Mutopo, P. (2014) *The Granary is Never Empty: Land Based Livelihoods and Female Transitory Mobility after Fast Track Land Reform in Mwenezi District, Zimbabwe*. Leiden, Brill.

Murisa, T. (2013) 'From Rhetoric to Policy Action: An Analysis of the Agricultural Policy Reform in Six African Countries' (available at www.trustafrica.org).

NEPAD (2003) 'Comprehensive Africa Agriculture Development Programme (CAADP)'. Pretoria, NEPAD.

Poole, N.D. and R. Msoni (2013) 'Commercialisation: A meta-approach for agricultural development among smallholder farmers in Africa?' *Food Policy*, 41, pp. 155-165.

Practical Action and PELUM (2005) 'The crisis in African agriculture: A more effective role for EC aid?' www.africanvoices.org.uk.

Richards, P. (1989) 'Agriculture as a performance', in R. Chambers, A. Pacey and L. Thrupp (eds), *Farmer First: Farmer Innovation and Agricultur-*

al Research. London, Intermediate Technology Publications.

Richards, P. (1993) 'Cultivation: knowledge or performance?' in M. Hobart (ed.), *An Anthropological Critique of Development: the Growth of Ignorance*. London, Routledge.

Schönfeldt, H.C. and N. Hall (2013) 'Capacity building in food composition for Africa', *Food Chemistry*, 140(3), pp. 513-519.

7

Resourcing Women's Rights in Francophone Africa

Hakima Abbas

Introduction

From 2009 to 2011, TrustAfrica embarked on a project called Enhancing Women's Dignity, funded through a grant from the Dutch Ministry of Foreign Affairs as part of the ministry's support for meeting UN Millennium Development Goal 3 (MDG3), to promote gender equality and empower women. This chapter explores the impact of this work, not as an evaluation but rather as an analysis of the strengths and gaps in the conceptualisation and implementation of the project as well as an exploration of its longer-term ripple effect and sustainability. The intention is to undertake a broader reflection on African philanthropy, TrustAfrica's positionality and the possibilities for just funding. Through a feminist and pan-Africanist lens, the chapter begins by establishing a conceptual framework around African philanthropy, resourcing, and transformative change for women's rights and gender justice. Second, using qualitative primary data and by analysing grant documents and other materials, the chapter seeks to understand the strategy, achievements and lessons of TrustAfrica's work on women's rights and dignity and to reflect on the impact and sustainability of the project on feminist and women's rights movements as well as on feminist transformative change. Finally, the chapter offers a critique and recommendations for future work that draw from the lessons of the Enhancing Women's Dignity project as well as from the possibilities inherent in the unique position and mandate of TrustAfrica.

Conceptual framework

Over the last seventy years, transformative change for women's rights and gender justice in Africa has been significant, though uneven. The African feminist movement has grown in size, scope and influence while in policy and practice, women's rights have been established as a cornerstone of development. Nevertheless, the patriarchy embedded in formal and informal institutions from the nation-state to community level, continue to impede the full realisation of African women's rights and gender justice. The systemic oppression of women, girls and other oppressed genders is compounded by the intersecting oppressions of class, ethnicity, religion, national status and ability, amongst others.

I talk throughout this chapter of women's rights and gender justice in acknowledgement of a feminist framework that recognises the non-binary character of sex, the social construction of gender and that the system of patriarchy impacts multiple genders including women, trans and intersex people. For the purposes of this chapter, I use a people-centered and pan-Africanist view of rights that foregrounds the interests of the people of Africa, advocates a self-determination framework and centralises the democratisation of rights, which Shivji (1989) frames as the 'right to organize'. While borrowing the anti-imperialist and rejection of neo-liberal ideology in Shivji's attempts to enhance the codification of the right to self-determination, the conceptualisation underlying my analysis and recommendations incorporate African feminist frameworks of self-determination left out of Shivji's approach.

Autonomous social movements are critical to transformative change. Social movements are not composed of one organisation or group, but are made up of several networked nodes in a constellation of actors driven by a shared vision and propelled by collective action. I use the term movement or social movement throughout this paper not to describe the informal organisation of large groups of people for political mobilisation as it is sometimes used, but to describe the sets of people, organisations, groups, collectives, constituents, intellectuals etc. that work towards a common political agenda over a period of time (Batliwala, 2008). Movements are important because they create the potential for sustained change by not only institutionalising reform but also by consolidating transformation by reshaping relations (people-ising change)

(Abbas, 2010). Movements are at the root of collective imagining of a just society and at the heart of turning that vision into reality. The literature on social movements is divided on which factors or strengths account for their influence and power. From my lived experiences with and within autonomous social movements throughout Africa, a fluid combination of interrelating and intersecting factors, rather than one alone, account for a movement's ability to realise change. What is more, any theoretical formula for impact is only an approximation for the messy reality of transformation. What is consistent is that social movements need clear political frames or ideologies, networks, identity, and material and non-material resources. In other words, social movements that create change are clear about their vision of a just world, able to draw others to this vision and allow others in turn to shape the collective vision; they are clear about their strategies for achieving new relations and are networked with others who share their political vision within a spectrum of frames; and finally their efforts are resourced with energy and material. Importantly, the local and global political, social and economic contexts within which movements engage play a significant role in the extent to which a social movement is able to collectivise the visioning of new power relations and mobilise action towards their vision.

In a global study on violence against women (VAW), Htun and Weldon (2012) showed that 'the autonomous mobilization of feminists in domestic and transnational contexts – not leftist parties, women in government, or national wealth – is the critical factor accounting for policy change'. The study demonstrated that feminist movements are the key political force in creating change in the policy and practice around violence against women. The authors note that violence against women is an issue that hits at the heart of patriarchy by challenging gender roles and cisgender male power defined by patriarchy. 'In the case of VAW, autonomous feminist movements are the primary drivers of change because they articulate social group perspectives, disseminate new ideas and frames to the broader public, and demand institutional changes that recognize these meanings.' (ibid.) The study further recognises that the role of autonomous social movements on the issue of VAW changes over time as dominant ideas and political frames shift in response to the movement's demands. As institutions encode policies to address violence against women, the role of autonomous social movements becomes important in ensuring that policy turns into practice and becomes the vehicle for people to appropriate and give normative meaning to these policies and laws.

The literature is less clear on women's political participation and its long-term impact on building a society free from gendered oppression. The theory that women in political power will transform the condition of women in general relies on the assumption that women in these positions will advance women's rights and gender justice while also instituting feminist policy in all areas. A 'critical mass' of women in governance, in turn, is expected to achieve systemic change in the political culture of representation and accountability (Batliwala, 2008; Hassim, 2010). However, as Nzomo (2015) notes: 'there persists unresolved structural impediments in the governance system, that are impervious, unresponsive and tend to block gender equality and democratic justice initiatives'. The patriarchy and colonial framework in the foundation of the structures and institutions of political systems in Africa begs the question whether transformation is possible from within these frameworks of power. McFadden (1992), referring to African nationalism as the foundation for state power, writes that 'nationalism can be understood as essentially a male defined and patriarchally rooted ideology which emerge[d] at a particular time in the history of a people, as a response to oppression and external domination'. McFadden argues that the insertion of individual women into these positions may, at best, narrowly challenge androcentric power in governance and at worst work against the demands of a feminist movement seeking to subvert patriarchy, among other axes of oppression. A concerted effort from many quarters to increase the number of women in political power and leadership across power bases, has led some to decry the exercise as a numbers game without substance, leading many feminists to see the tactic of increasing women's political participation and leadership as only one part of a broader strategy to subvert the norms and practices of state power. One response is the building of a feminist base of 'leaders' with access to political power working as part of, in concert with and accountable to the feminist movement across the continent.

Engaging different terrains of struggle, the state being one of them, without privileging it as the sole site for change-making, has the potential in the short term to enable and support feminist movement demands and to shift the dominant culture of these systems. As Nzomo (2015) notes: 'This entails paying more attention to the process and criteria of selecting political leaders and setting enforceable accountability mechanisms for holding accountable political office seekers and power holders. It also requires gender champions and committed democrats to eliminate the patriarchal institutional norms and values that normalize inequalities and undermine the advancement of gender and democratic agendas, and the enforcement of accountability mechanisms.' However, whether this strategy will also enable the demise of the very governance systems which are being used, and the renewal of direct democracy, remains to be seen.

Social movements shift power when they exist in their totality – the full spectrum of formations – rather than as a single formation or sub-grouping. However, organisations (and typically non-governmental organisations) and in some instances even individuals have been the primary targets of the growing funding sector. This focus on organisations has shifted the locus of change for many movements, sometimes fragmenting and siloing different expressions of peoples' resistance or alternative building and centreing power in professionalised, often urban, organisations. Conversely, the over-reliance on the funding sector to resource civil society has left many organisations, and even movements, vulnerable to funding shifts and external agendas. To understand these dynamics one must also understand the diversity of the funding sector. A whole industry has flourished globally to distribute financial resources for civil society. It is composed of a myriad of actors from multilateral and bilateral agencies to corporate philanthropy and private philanthropy.

Philanthropy in Africa is at times simplistically understood to consist of charity or the aid architecture, which most troublingly is centred on a narrative of the global north helping Africa. This narrative is ahistorical and, as I have argued elsewhere, reinforces the very asymmetry of power that needs addressing to shift the root causes of global inequalities and impoverishment (Abbas, 2009). A deeper look at African philanthropy gives a much wider understanding of the ways in which resources are generated, transmitted and collectivised for social good, if not for social change, in the continent. Bhekinkosi Moyo (2010) attempts to create a framework for African philanthropy that embraces the lifelong dynamics of benefitting and bestowing from African collective support systems both new and old. He argues that most Africans are themselves philanthropists and that the social fabric of African societies has been woven across time on the basis of mutual exchange between individuals and collectives. New forms of philanthropy continue then to be shaped by new forms of need. However, the question remains as to how these exchanges of resources, material and non-material, can be put to use to shift systemic oppressions. Indeed, it is clear that just and sustainable societies will be built in Africa only with our own knowledges and our own resources (Moyo and Ramsamy, 2014). Given that resources yield agenda-setting power, their distribution cannot be dictated by people or entities removed from the contexts and with interests that may or may not align with those of African peoples.

Formally institutionalised African philanthropic entities are re-sourced in different ways. Some obtain all of their funding from local sources. Others have a mix of local and international sources and yet others rely predominantly on funding from the global North. While African resources (material as well as non-material) will certainly be the leverage of African transformation, little scholarship has emerged to significantly attest to the impact of African philanthropy and fund-ing engines in comparison to those of Northern-led entities. Empirical evidence suggests that African philanthropic vehicles provide more opportunities to determine priorities based on need because of their proximity to the societies and contexts they are attempting to support and therefore their ability to make more informed and relevant choic-es. Indeed, this logic is not limited to African foundations, but also to the array of women's, LGBTIQ, youth and other funds that serve and lead particular movements and constituencies, examples of which include Mama Cash, FRIDA and the African Women's Development Fund. These foundations have made innovative and creative attempts at ensuring that their agendas are indeed responsive to the needs of their constituencies rather than those of their funding sources by using participatory funding approaches including peer grant making mech-anisms and constituency leadership in their governance, staffing, etc. Importantly, one of the distinctions between these funds and the, of-ten larger, funding sources from outside of the movements, is the ideo-logical base of their approach, in the case of women's funds, resting on feminist principles, and in the case of some African funds, resting on the principles of pan-Africanism.

Nevertheless, a strong critique of the current model of African foun-dations is that they often remain as pass-through vehicles for North-ern-based resources due to the fact that they themselves in some in-stances are vulnerable to Northern funding trends and priorities, thus limiting their power or positionality to determine their own priorities. Unfortunately, philanthropy of all kinds have been plagued by the same model inherited by Northern funding approaches that attempt to fix the symptoms of systemic oppression without radically transforming the system itself, a necessary feat deemed by some funding actors to be controversial. As Bhekinkosi Moyo suggests 'the geographic location alone doesn't change the dynamic of a donor, conditions apply even when the donor is African. What we must do is generate our own income.'[1] Despite these challenges and learning, community-based, movement-led and other African foundations have been well received by African actors across the board and have been steadily growing in number, scope and scale.

Despite the need for significant shifts to guarantee the rights of Africa's women and girls and the centrality of women's rights and feminist movements to achieve this change, this movement continues to be severely under-resourced. This trend is, however, not only localised in Africa; the funding landscape for women's and girls' rights and development has historically been sorely lacking throughout the world and across financing sectors. A 2010 global survey conducted by the Association for Women's Rights in Development (AWID) found that, of the 740 women's rights organisations surveyed, the median annual income was just $20,000 a year. Of these organisations, 48% had never received core funding and 52% had never received multi-year funding. In Africa, excluding the countries of North Africa, AWID's research found that the median income of women's rights organisations was significantly less than the global median at just $12,136 annually, thus signaling a severely under-resourced movement.

It is important to note that feminists stress the importance not only of the amount of funding but the quality of funding necessary to sustain feminist activism and movements. Quality of funding refers to the ability of multiple types of formations within a movement (i.e. collectives, groups, associations, academics, organisations etc.) to access funds through open, transparent and contextually accessible processes that do not dictate their work or priorities. Core funding that allows for organisational or institutional building, sustainability and resilience is also a key element of quality funding. Linked to this, multi-year (preferably medium- to long-term) flexible funding is a critical ingredient to enable and accompany movement formations through processes of transformation which tend to be non-linear, require learning and shifts, and take significant time (Clark, et al., 2006).

---

1 Interviewed by the author on 7 June 2016.

The MDG3 Fund

In 2000, the UN General Assembly adopted the Millennium Development Goals (MDGs) in an attempt to set time-bound goals to commitments on development. Many critics of the MDGs rightly pointed out that they set bare minimum standards, reduced development to an apolitical process by ignoring the systemic causes of inequalities that are deep rooted and intrinsic to global capitalist systems, and were adopted without popular dialogue, consultation or participation to be imposed, for the large part, on the global South. While goal 3 of the MDGs enshrined gender equality in its own right and as necessary for development, feminist critiques went further to point out that (i) the MDGs failed to recognise, and rather reduced and diluted, existing commitments on gender equality, (ii) failed to make gender a cross-cutting theme across all goals, and (iii) were devoid of a human rights framework and reduced systemic economic inequality inherent in the aid, debt, trade and global financial architecture to a request for increased donor assistance (Barton, 2004).

In Africa, the predictions of the pitfalls and opportunities related to the MDGs came to fruition. While the goals were minimalist, African states on the whole struggled to attain them: some much needed attention and important gains were made in relation to some of the goals, while others remained mostly unfulfilled. Civil society critiqued the goals and the lack of participation in the drafting process but played an important role in turning the goals into reality by providing services and making relevant demands on power holders. The African feminist and women's rights movement in particular engaged the goals in formal and non-formal ways, not only focusing on the three goals widely considered gender-related (goal 3 on gender equality, goal 5 on maternal mortality and goal 10 on HIV/Aids) but also adopting and gendering the other goals through various campaigns and other actions. This engagement by civil society created the necessary adaptation to contextual realities and therefore potential popular ownership of the goals' aims, while ensuring that the reductionist agenda wasn't the end but rather a means. This was evident for example in the pan-African maternal mortality campaigns led by the Solidarity for African Women's Rights (SOAWR) coalition that invoked goal 5 while also stressing the obligations made within the Maputo Protocol[2] and other international commitments.

---

2   See: http://www.achpr.org/instruments/women-protocol/

Immediately evident in the MDG process was the need for the goals to be resourced. While many accompanying processes and commitments on financing for development were aligned to the MDGs, as AWID's research states, 'it was clear that none of them were likely to be achieved unless the world's rich nations, and bilateral, multilateral and private funding agencies, committed serious resources to their realization' (Batliwala et al., 2013). This was particularly true for the women's rights and gender equality related goals where women's rights and feminist movements are severely under resourced. Bearing this in mind, and during a moment of consultations on the future of Dutch development cooperation in 2007, there was 'recognition that abolishing the stand-alone budget for women's rights and gender equality in the early years of the new Millennium had not been a wise decision' (IOB, 2015). As was acknowledged in these consultations, the rise in fundamentalist opposition to women's rights and gender justice in the global South and the severe under-resourcing of feminist and women's rights movements were creating a situation where even the minimal goals of the MDGs would be mere aspirations.

In an attempt to redress this lack of funding, the Dutch Ministry of Development Cooperation created an €82 million global MDG3 Fund in 2008 that specifically targeted the realisation of women and girls' rights; it was the largest fund ever created specifically directed at civil society working on women and girls' rights. The awards were given to 45 projects or institutions around the world through an open and competitive process in a grant cycle of about three years. The fund was built around four themes: securing property and inheritance rights for women, increasing women's participation in politics and public administration, promoting employment and equal employment opportunities, and ending violence against women and girls. However, the themes were loosely interpreted, allowing a wide range of funding partners to secure the resources. Two-thirds of the funds were provided to Southern-based organisations and a significant portion to re-granting organisations, including women's funds, in an attempt to multiply the reach and impact of the funds (IOB, 2015). As AWID's evaluation of the MDG3 fund overall observes 'by supporting a number of women's funds, community foundations, human rights funds, and women's organizations with re-granting functions, the Fund has helped to channel much needed resources to over 3,600 small, community-based women's organizations … [that undertook] critical interventions for grassroots women's awareness, empowerment, mobilization, and assertion of their rights' (Batliwala et al., 2013).

Enhancing women's dignity: An analysis

TrustAfrica was one of the intermediary organisations that received funding from the MDG3 Fund to implement the Enhancing Women's Dignity project. At the time, TrustAfrica's programme had three pillars: democracy and civil society, an area of work across the continent that sought to create the conditions for citizen participation; equitable development, which sought to respond to the economic conditions on the continent; and philanthropy as a means of resourcing movements for the other two objectives to be achieved. The programmatic work was multi-stakeholder in the sense that it created links and bridges between civil society, policy makers, the private sector and the funding community.

Having been awarded a three-year grant of €992,700 in 2009 from the MDG3 fund, TrustAfrica provided grants through the Enhancing Women's Dignity project to 19 organisations and networks working on women's political leadership or on violence against women and girls (or both) in seven Francophone countries of West and Central Africa. TrustAfrica documents reflect that the project design of the intervention was deliberate and holistic, including leadership development, capacity building, research, network building and funding. However, the theory of change of the project was not precise and its outcomes not as concrete and specific as would be necessary to achieve longer-term impact. In fact, this critique seems to have been leveled similarly at the MDG3 fund more globally. According to the independent evaluation conducted by IOB: 'In its design of the [MDG3] Fund, the ministry adopted a project approach but without a clear overall programme strategy (currently referred to as "theory of change") of what milestones would be needed to realise the overall objective of realising *"concrete improvements in rights and opportunities for women and girls in developing countries in Africa, Latin America and Asia"'* (IOB, 2015; emphasis in original).

The organisations receiving the funds through TrustAfrica's Enhancing Women's Dignity fund employed various tactics in their work, including knowledge generation and research, capacity-building, awareness-raising, advocacy and lobbying, as well as participatory media, art and communications. The organisations were diverse in terms of their reach and scope: CAFOB, in Burundi, was a national network with membership throughout the country; CRIGED, in Burkina Faso, had a presence largely in the capital; CLVF, in Senegal, had field offices throughout the country, and others, like FEMNET Mali, were regional or national offices of larger pan-African organisations or networks. Not all of the organisations had specific feminist or women's rights mandates and missions, nor were all women-led, though the majority did and were.

There was an attempt in each country to fund at least two organisations and to ensure that each addressed at least one of the priority issues (women's participation in political leadership and violence against women and girls). It is important to note that violence against women and girls was approached broadly, and included supporting work against female genital mutilation, sexual and gender-based violence in schools, and access to services and medical care for women or girls in need of fistula repair. Similarly, the approach to women's political participation didn't solely focus on women in politics. As Codou Bop of GREFELS, one of the grantee partners, noted: 'we addressed a central question in the citizenship of women, which is the registration of girls. Without birth certificates, they are invisible and cannot enjoy any of their rights as citizens, let alone the opportunity to run for elected office or to elect candidates. These activities took place in rural areas and specifically targeted young women who showed interest in politics. Another remarkable aspect of the project was the use by young women of community media, broadcasting in national languages, particularly community radio.'[3] The inclusion of young women as constituents in the portfolio is noteworthy, as it potentially contributes to shifting the locus of knowledge and power, which tend to be centralised in older generations in African feminist movements. Diversity also existed in relation to the organisations' annual budgets, with some struggling for funds while others had a stable multi-year income. Similarly, the portfolio mix ranged from an organisation established that same year to one that was over 20 years old.

Despite this diversity, support was offered only to NGOs and not to other formations within civil society. As I noted above, in order to shift violence against women and enhance women's political leadership in Africa, systemic change needs to be led by diverse movement actors. For this reason, funders looking to contribute to such transformative change must consider supporting an ecosystem of movement actors working

---

3   Interviewed by the author on 2 August 2016.

from different spheres of struggle and in a variety of formations over the longer term to respond to the gains, losses, shifting roles and targets to accomplish this change. My interviews with former TrustAfrica staff members suggest that the capacity of the foundation to grant to non-registered organisations or other types of formations is limited by its institutional policies. However, in respect to the MDG3 fund specifically, given the vastness of the region covered, the diversity of tactics employed and the limited resources, this limitation may not have had a significant effect on the potential for impact of the portfolio across movements. Another mitigating factor may have been the engagement of informal and formal institutions and sites of power by several of the NGOs funded. Examples include working within community structures and institutions to shift attitudes, or with state structures to shift policy and laws.

TrustAfrica's funding was also important given the fact that social justice movements in francophone countries are severely under-funded. Headquartered in Dakar, Senegal, TrustAfrica has made significant steps in rectifying this, and in ensuring a multilingual approach. Few large foundations have a mandate, significant funding portfolios or offices in the regions. Women's rights organisations and networks there tend to receive most of their funds from bilateral or multilateral organisations such as the Organisation internationale de la Francophonie and the Canadian International Development Agency, while others receive theirs from smaller, more specialised funds such as the New Field Foundation. Mama Cash and the African Women's Development Fund are two women's funds which have had longer engagement in the region and have provided important core and project based funding to women's rights organisations, groups and networks. The fact that TrustAfrica's Enhancing Women's Dignity project contributed to filling an important gap in the funding landscape made it a significant intervention with the promise of important impact. Yves Niyiragira of Fahamu[4] also emphasised this key contribution: 'TrustAfrica funding in francophone countries was important as organizations in these countries are not on the radar of many donors, particularly those in countries such as Cameroun, Niger and Mali. The project funded in these countries.'

A related achievement of TrustAfrica's intervention, is the creation of a network of women's organisations working on VAW in francophone Africa (Batliwala et al., 2013). As Akwasi Aidoo, TrustAfrica's founding

---

4   Interviewed by the author on 24 March 2016.

executive director, contends, TrustAfrica is in 'the business of making a forest out of trees and building a dense ecosystem of organizations, communities, and borderless fields' (Barya and Richardson, 2012). In order to achieve this networked community, TrustAfrica included in the design of the Enhancing Women's Dignity project, annual workshops for grantees to learn new skills and share lessons and strategies. The project also set up a listserv and blog to maintain communication across grantees. Unfortunately, the network of grantees does not seem to have been sustained beyond the life cycle of the project in any formal sense, perhaps because of over-reliance on TrustAfrica, and the poor ICT permeation in the regions. As Fahamu's Yves Niyiragira argues: 'The email group or blog didn't survive because we didn't explore what we could work on together and how that joint work could be resourced. They didn't start with the work.'[5] However, Niyiragira feels that Fahamu played some role in expanding the networks available to the grantees and reckons that TrustAfrica was correct to include them in the portfolio for that reason. As he notes: 'part of our funding was to strengthen the access of the other grantees to the African Union. We did this by working through the SOAWR coalition, which we were already a part of. In the end, two organizations in the TrustAfrica portfolio from Cameroun and Mali became members of SOAWR'.[6] It is beyond this chapter's scope to assess whether an informal network amongst the organisations has been created and whether previously existing relationships were strengthened through the project. It may be pertinent for TrustAfrica's future project design to explore whether any collective action or joint work was taken up nationally between the pairs of organisations in the grantee cohort or across geographies with those working on similar themes and whether the project led to deepened connectivity nationally, regionally or across the continent.

The Enhancing Women's Dignity project began with knowledge building, with the thought that it had the potential for long-term use and value for multiple uses within the movement, including securing further funding. Thus the project focused on the production of knowledge about the capacities, agendas and lessons learned of women's rights organisations, and documentation of the stories of women changemakers. Karima Grant Abbott of ImagiNation Afrika, who ran the capacity building and leadership development workshops of the initiative, notes

---

5   Interviewed by the author on 24 March 2016.
6   Interviewed by the author on 24 March 2016.

that the research component was important, as 'it put the work in context'. Indeed, the documentation of feminist knowledge, realities and analysis is key to enabling the type of power analysis needed to create meaningful change. Examples of these outputs included a database of women's rights organisations, the profiles of 'women leaders' and an illustrated training manual on communications and strategic advocacy.[7] Although these outputs are available online, with the exception of the database, none seem to have been widely disseminated beyond the project grantees, a seemingly lost opportunity for feminist knowledge generation and learning. Nevertheless, TrustAfrica's policy of beginning portfolios by generating knowledge, usually through convenings, on the context and priorities of the movement allows for movement-led grant making. As Sandra Zerbo, formerly of TrustAfrica and programme officer for the project, noted regarding the funds for Enhancing Women's Dignity: 'What we did with the money is what was needed.'[8] Indeed, as she suggests, funding priorities were determined by the priorities of the movement through the knowledge building process and the work done with grantees in the application process. Similarly, TrustAfrica remained attuned and flexible to changing realities and unforeseen priorities as the grantees interviewed for this chapter attested. On the flip side, this model also means not accepting unsolicited proposals, which in turn runs the risk of approaching the movement ecosystem too narrowly. Moreover, while this approach suggests a potential shift from externally driven priorities, it also creates a framework for project-driven funding rather than funding that is based on movement support and strategy and that offers core and long-term support – key elements of quality funding.

TrustAfrica provided project-specific funding for organisations in the Enhancing Women's Dignity portfolio. Yves Niyiragira reports appreciating the flexibility, discussion and advice on the projects to be implemented, as well as the relative ease of the application and reporting processes. And while grantees were allowed to include overhead or core support in their budgets, it appears that this was only in the region of 10% of the total grant. AWID's research suggests that best practice funding for women's rights necessitates a much larger portion of core sup-

---

7   This manual is permanently archived on IssueLab at http://www.issuelab. org/resource/women_s_political_participation_training_manual_communication_ and_strategic_advocacy

8   Interviewed by the author on 28 July 2016.

port over the long term (Clark et al., 2006). The MDG3 grant cycle was three years, but the Enhancing Women's Dignity grants seem to have been distributed on an annual cycle. A three-year commitment would have been of significant value for many organisations whose income is often determined on a year-to-year basis and whose work attempts to shift entrenched norms and systems. Indeed, Niyiragira noted that the year-to-year funding cycle was disruptive and created uncertainty that made it difficult for organisations to make long-term projections. While acknowledging this ideal, TrustAfrica staff note that the project design did not build in the timeframes needed for TrustAfrica to make the initial medium term commitment to the grantee partners.[9] Multi-year core funding is key to ensuring the long-term viability of systemic change for women's rights and gender justice in Africa. Women's rights organisations need to be able to sustain campaigns, projects and initiatives as well as their own organisational development in order to build the necessary networks and strategies for systemic transformation. Resources need to be replenished and flexible in order for change to be maintained, intensified and adapted to the lessons learned of the intervention and changing contexts. Indeed, one of the limitations of grant making globally is that organisations are limited to dealing with the current context and realities, playing the proverbial role of firefighter, and not given the time and resources to design innovative projects that could enable them to develop their visions and create new realities – the difference between resisting and building. As Karima Grant Abbott said: 'I wonder if funding and funders like TrustAfrica can come in earlier and give women-led organisations a good amount of time and resources to design with their communities, across their organisations, to innovate, plot and plan together'.[10] The potential of such a design would be collective impact and leveraging collective power.

Aware of the three-year cycle of the MDG3 funds, TrustAfrica built into the project discussions on sustainable resourcing, including creative strategies such as crowdfunding. Project documents do not indicate the prior existence amongst TrustAfrica MDG3 grantees of funding models outside of seeking grants from multilateral or bilateral agencies and foundations, with the exception of the Association Nigérienne pour le Progrès et la Défense des Droits de la Femme (ANPDDF) in Niger, which collects dues from its membership. The project attempt-

---

9   Interviewed by the author on 28 July 2016.
10   Interviewed by the author on 24 March 2016.

ed to support diversification of funding for example through a creative crowdfunding campaign led by TrustAfrica for HEAL Africa. The project accompaniment and capacity building also enabled grantees access to UN agencies such as UN Women and UNDP, and included a fundraising workshop led by the African Women's Development Fund, thus leveraging TrustAfrica's social and political capital in the service of its grantees. It is not clear how many organisations were able to sustain the projects beyond the availability of TrustAfrica funding. However, there is no available indication that grantees implemented new methods of resource mobilisation following the grant cycle.

Importantly, TrustAfrica was not able to continue a partnership with the majority of organisations in the project beyond the availability of the MDG3 funds. This is despite internal discussions exploring the possibility of making these issues an organisational focus to allow for 'a more sustained approach and continuation of the project's work beyond June 2011', as expressed in a 2010 interim project report. TrustAfrica made an important choice in funding feminist and women's rights organisations in West and Central Africa but the resources should have been maintained if real change was to be sustained. The dedicated support for women's rights and gender justice may have been discontinued by TrustAfrica because this focus was not initially in their strategy, but was rather a consequence of TrustAfrica's successful application for the Dutch MDG3 fund. This speaks to the limitation of donor-led priorities and their sustainability.

Ultimately, despite TrustAfrica's desire to engage on women's rights at its core, this has not translated into significant funding for women's rights organisations across its portfolios, and TrustAfrica has not succeed in raising further funding for similar support. TrustAfrica might have continued women's rights and gender justice movement building in the region by ensuring that its own capacities were developed during the period of the project to use a women's rights and feminist lens across its work. The foundation might also have considered creating partnerships with women's funds in Africa for joint work on a particular theme. Indeed, many of the issues currently being addressed by the work of TrustAfrica have significant gendered impacts and could benefit from the knowledge and analysis from this perspective. Women's organisations and initiatives are part of TrustAfrica's early learning and agriculture advocacy portfolios, but women have only recently come into focus across the board of other portfolios, such as the work on illicit financial flows. A former staff member suggests that TrustAfrica might have considered a gender policy or strategy formulation that ensured the continuation of funding for gender justice and women's rights by guaranteeing the allocation of a portion of budget funds to women-led organisations or women's rights work. This policy might also extend to the internal working of the foundation, such as procurement and research policies.

Nevertheless, the sustainability of the impact of the Enhancing Women's Dignity project is also possibly embedded in the accompanying work done during the funding cycle. Through the project, TrustAfrica provided leadership and capacity building for grantees which allowed peer-to-peer learning and exchange as well as skills and knowledge building. According to Karima Grant Abbott, 'there is an inherent power in bringing African women together. The women in the TrustAfrica group were deeply engaged and made full use of the space provided them, the rare opportunity to be together, to reflect and to learn; they turned every workshop into work sessions, immediately applying what they were learning and digging deep into the learning to draw what they could for their work. They fully grasped the potential impact for them to develop better organisations.'[11]

Examples of this included training on African human rights frameworks like the Protocol on the Rights of Women in Africa, support for the participation of grantees in African Union summits where they could advocate for policy changes, and the targeted and customised advocacy assistance to 14 grantees. Grant Abbott said that TrustAfrica staff understood that resourcing for movement building goes beyond funding, to include a transformative leadership training approach: 'TrustAfrica really invested resources in designing a process that used a systems approach and looked at what are the principles behind what we do, what are the lessons we draw and what drives change.'[12]

While an initiative's successes should not depend on individuals alone, but on institutions more broadly, those interviewed for this chapter singled out Sandra Zerbo as a young African woman with strong capacities, vision and feminist analysis. She was known to be accessible, committed and a valuable resource to grantees, and her leadership enabled a shift in donor and grantee interaction to a relationship of trust and support. Karima Grant Abbot noted: 'The women were excited to be in a different space, to engage differently with a donor, to feel respected

11   Interviewed by the author on 24 March 2016.
12   Interviewed by the author on 24 March 2016.

by a donor... TrustAfrica were very ethical, engaged and committed. This was evident when other staff of the foundation also attended one of the trainings, including the leadership, and gave space to listen and learn.'[13]

Conclusion

As I mention in the introduction, this chapter is by no means an external evaluation of the Enhancing Women's Dignity initiative, nor does it profess to come to absolute conclusions about the work that was done. Rather, it is a basis for analysis and reflection of the realities and potential of an African-led fund in supporting change for women's rights and gender justice.

TrustAfrica's mandate and vision remain acutely relevant in a world with ever shrinking democratic and civil society space and in a continent still struggling to attain the aspirations of social, economic, political and environmental justice. The manifestations of multiple forms of fascism and anti-rights ideologies in Africa find common ground with sustaining patriarchy. The logic of domination targets women and LGBTIQ communities in particular but intersects with multiple forms of domination that perpetuate impoverishment and keep the aspirations of liberation elusive for all. In this moment, the need for a strong continental feminist movement that is able to tackle oppression and build visions of freedom is essential. Organised political change is possible through women's rights NGOs, trade unions, farmer and peasant associations, political parties, policymakers and academics. This movement will need to be resourced and networked – a role that TrustAfrica can play with significant impact if it maintains its vision of being a pan-African fund, generating and redistributing resources, with connectedness to the movements it serves. Quality resourcing will also demand long-term core support that is responsive to the changing context and role of the movement.

Sandra Zerbo elaborated some of the key strengths of TrustAfrica: 'Interpretation of the landscape, the flexibility to change course, the use and ethics of re-granting and the attention to the outputs and outcomes of grants.'[14] Current funding and movement architectures, and their uncertainty, maintain a level of patronage that will only shift with a deep change in mindsets and systems. A social justice agenda is one that re-

---

13   Interviewed by the author on 24 March 2016.
14   Interviewed by the author on 28 July 2016.

quires risk and vision, which are not necessarily a priority for many corporations, donors and individuals with access to large amounts of money who often prefer to address the shorter term symptoms of injustice rather than the systems that perpetuate it. However, social justice as an agenda has the potential to be popular, and leveraging collective peoples' power can be a way to correct the imbalance between those who hold the purse strings and those who believe in redistribution of resources. In this sense, the project design, relationships built and care taken in the detailed implementation of the Enhancing Women's Dignity project point to TrustAfrica's commitment to shifting the locus of power and patronage of dominant funding landscapes. In the ten years that TrustAfrica has been in existence, it has successfully built important social and political capital with a range of African and global actors. This success is not to be minimised. Accompanied in the next ten years by a significant endowment and independent resources, this combination of capital, and the framework within TrustAfrica for it to be leveraged in the service of movement building, could be a game changer in Africa.

However, as many of the interviewees noted, in the long term TrustAfrica's success will depend on the foundation's ability to become financially independent and sustainable. It is important to note that TrustAfrica has yet to have a long-term strategy funded by a set of donors, and that some of its recent large portfolios such the Enhancing Women's Dignity project and the Early Learning portfolio, were responses to donor calls rather than originating from a long-term strategy. While TrustAfrica still relies on international donors for much of its income, a critical component of the fund's potential to provide flexible core funding for social justice activists, groups, organisations and collectives will be its ability to generate and control African resources and create a significant endowment. This is indeed key to the foundation's own sustainability and resilience, as well as to its ability to be independent and autonomous.

To achieve women's rights and gender justice in Africa will require profound change being built piece by piece by the many feminist movements and actors across the continent using an array of tactics. Normative and systemic change will require an intersectional analysis and substantial resources. In fact, any agenda for social justice in Africa that doesn't include these will be unable to make the inroads that our continent, context and social justice aspirations require. TrustAfrica, throughout its work, must ensure that women's rights and gender justice are at the heart of its mandate and that a feminist framework is used throughout the work, in the power and impact analyses, in setting priorities, in grant making, in knowledge building, and in internal mechanisms and ways of working. As TrustAfrica celebrates its 10th anniversary, the foundation must also reflect on its successes and challenges and steer the organisational boat towards the next ten years with a firm commitment in principle and practice to the centrality of women's rights and gender justice to achieve its vision of a just Africa.

References

Abbas, H. (2010) 'The revolution will not be funded: The role of donors in the movement for social justice in Africa'. Pambazuka News, 17 November.

Abbas, H. with N. Ndeda (2009) 'Aid and reparations: power in the development discourse' in H. Abbas and Y. Niyiragira (eds) *Aid to Africa: Redeemer or Coloniser?* Cape Town, Pambazuka Press.

Barton, C. (2004) 'Women's Movements and Gender Perspectives on the Millennium Development Goals', in *Civil Society Perspectives on the Millennium Development Goals*. New York, UNDP Civil Society Unit.

Barya, M.K. and W. Richardson (2012) *TrustAfrica: A Chronicle*, p. 16 Available at http://trustafrica.org/en/about-us/our-history. Accessed August 9, 2016.

Batliwala, S. (2008) 'Changing Their World: Concepts and Practices of Women's Movements'. Toronto, Association for Women's Rights in Development.

Batliwala, S. with S. Rosenhek and J. Miller (2013) 'Women Moving Mountains: Collective Impact of the Dutch MDG3 Fund. How Resources Advance Women's Rights and Gender Equality'. Toronto, Association for Women's Rights in Development.

Clark, C., E. Sprenger, and L. VeneKlasen of Just Associates, in collaboration with Lydia Alpizar Duran and Joanna Kerr of AWID (2006) 'Where is the money for women's rights? Assessing resources and the role of donors in the promotion of women's rights and the support of women's rights organizations'. Toronto, Association for Women's Rights in Development.

Hassim, S. (2010) 'Perverse consequences? The impact of quotas for women on democratisation in Africa', in I. Shapiro, S.C. Stokes, E.J. Wood and A.S. Kirshner (eds), *Political Representation*. Cambridge, Cambridge University Press.

Htun, M. and S. Laurel Weldon (2012) The Civic Origins of Progressive Policy Change: Combating Violence against Women in Global Perspective, 1975-2005', *American Political Science Review*, 106(3), pp. 548569.

McFadden, P. (1992) 'Nationalism and Gender Issues in South Africa', *Journal of Gender Studies*, 1(4), pp. 510-520.

Moyo, B. (2010) 'Philanthropy in Africa: functions, status, challenges and opportunities', in N. MacDonald and L. de Borms (eds) *Global Philanthropy*. London, MF Publishing.

Moyo, B. and K. Ramsamy (2014) 'African philanthropy, pan-Africanism, and Africa's development', *Development in Practice*, 24(5-6), pp. 656-671.

Nzomo, M. (2015) 'Women and Political Governance in Africa: A Feminist Perspective', *Pathways to African Feminism and Development*, Journal of African Women's Studies Centre, 1(1).

IOB Evaluation (2015) 'Evaluation of the MDG3 Fund 'Investing in Equality' (2008-2011)'. Dutch Ministry of Foreign Affairs.

Issa Shivji (1989) The Concept of Human Rights in Africa, Dakar, Codesria.

8

Re-imagining Agency in Africa

Tendai Murisa

Introduction

The continent has in the past three decades gone through what we commonly refer to as the 'winds of change' – shorthand for the transitions from one-party states and military dictatorships to multi-party political systems. The changes were mostly driven by ordinary citizens. It was one of the loudest statements made by Africans concerning their aspirations for a more just political order, and it benefitted from the collapse of the former Soviet Union: African politics was geared for significant and unprecedented change after the end of the bipolar world.

This chapter examines, from an insider's view, the basis upon which TrustAfrica has acted over the past decade, and reflects broadly on our contributions. The second half of the chapter is largely based on strategic work within the organisation about what we think will deepen African agency and contribute towards moving the needle on a number of issues currently inhibiting the achievement of political and socio-economic justice on the continent.

Significance of the winds of change

Beginning in the early 1990s, pro-democracy movements – sustained mostly by labour unions – emerged across the continent demanding constitutional reforms to allow for multi-party democracy. Unlike in other regions, however, there was a missing piece in the equation – thriving civil society institutions working to mediate the rapid changes taking place. Although our continent was and remains very association-al in nature, we did not have an adequate infrastructure to cope with the complex challenges that attempts at democratisation and economic liberalisation were about to throw at us. All of a sudden we had new so-ciety-wide obligations and responsibilities, for instance around civic ed-ucation to ensure that democracy can become a lived reality. We had to concern ourselves about how we would be organising elections, through voter-education and election monitoring, for instance, as the sitting gov-ernment could not be trusted with such responsibility. We also needed non-state organisations that could defend human rights and also en-sure that state excesses are curtailed. Although we had democratised we learnt through the experiences of others that state-based political elites could not be left to exercise power alone. Most of us in Africa knew by then that the temptation for abuse of office is always high and can only be curtailed through ongoing public scrutiny.

We were suddenly confronted with the withdrawal of the African state from the provision of public goods which had been described as in-efficient and too bureaucratic to deliver development. In fact, although the 'winds of change' specifically referred to changes within the politi-cal systems we also experienced these winds within the socio-economic space through the adoption of the Bretton Woods Institutions imposed Structural Adjustment Programs (SAPs) which literally marked the end of any romantic notions of socialism but instead saw most of us adopt-ing market oriented reforms under what has been referred to as the Washington Consensus.[1] We had to think of new ways of re-organising the delivery of public goods such as education, health and sanitation, and also dealing with new problems such rapid urbanisation.

Although there are many actors within what can be called broadly civil society it was the emergence of a thriving NGO sector that was both spectacular and significant in many ways. It gave us a new way of doing things and also the hope that citizen based formations could respond to the new challenges. Although NGOs were new,[2] and many were small

1   The term Washington Consensus was coined in 1989 by economist John Wil-liamson to describe a set of specific economic policy prescriptions that constituted the 'standard' reform package promoted for crisis-wrecked developing countries by Washington, D.C.-based institutions such as the IMF, World Bank, and the US Treasury Department. The prescriptions encompassed policies in such areas as macroeconomic stabilisation, economic opening with respect to both trade and investment, and the expansion of market forces within the domestic economy.

2   NGOs have been active Africa since the 1950s but had mostly played a peripheral

in size, we welcomed the possibility of their creating new opportunities for engaging with the state.

TrustAfrica: catalysing agency

When TrustAfrica was established in 2006 we were fortunate enough to find a vibrant civil society spread – albeit unevenly – across Africa. Both the board and the staff of TrustAfrica were made up of people who had invested time and experience in this civil society, and so the organisation quickly benefitted from the already existing networks and relationships. We committed ourselves to working alongside a broad movement comprising NGOs, membership associations and unions, policy oriented think tanks and other grant-making institutions. We saw civil society as the arena in which the rights of citizens would be defended, the power of political elites be subjected to some modicum of discipline, and the function of markets be given public scrutiny. This would be the place where history was made.

From the inception we were very clear about our mission: as an institution steeped in the centuries-old traditions of African philanthropy we would model interventions through partnership and nurturing ties of solidarity aimed at strengthening civil society to achieve the twin goals of democracy and development. We have since then worked to resolve policy-embedded challenges such as gender inequity and patriarchy, systemic violence and oppression of citizens by the yesteryear liberators, addressing the transformation challenge within smallholder agriculture, growing concerns about impunity, improving prospects for domestic resource mobilisation by curtailing illicit financial flows and also nurturing African philanthropy. Ours was also an attempt to promote initiatives led by Africans, informed by an objective appreciation of the continent's social, economic and political context. We hoped that our work would contribute towards reaffirming confidence in the agency of Africans seeking solutions to the continent's most endemic problems. We placed our bet on civil society in its broader manifestation, and saw it as a space where deficits in our democracies and development could be addressed.

There are five areas that have been particularly exciting for us as an organisation: achieving the mission of enhancing citizen-based agency for democracy and development, ensuring that we are credible land-

---

welfare role. In the new dispensation they had to take a more prominent role in both service delivery and advocacy.

scape interpreters, understanding our partners (civil society), the supply-chain (philanthropy) and reflecting more on how we have worked and what we could have done differently. We were very clear from the beginning that there was no silver bullet that would resolve Africa's challenges. Instead, we would need to invest in catalytic initiatives whose impact would be felt well beyond our initial efforts.

In our first strategy document we clarified our role as that of catalyst and collaborator. We stated that we would '… foster dialogue, and support projects that address Africa's democratic and developmental challenges … by strengthen[ing] the capacities of civil society organisations to be more effective and to secure the democratic space in which they operate'.[3] This was based on the conviction that a vibrant civil society was a necessary component of the democracy and development equation. As already mentioned, the continent had just made the shift to more democratic and civilian governments than at any other time in the last century. It was indeed a moment of great hope for the continent, but even then we realised the need for a vibrant civil society effectively engaged in speaking truth to power and continuously exposing the excesses of governments. We sought to defend the new realities and ensure that the people of Africa benefit from the transition to civilian and democratic governments. We were also not alone, for there were credible voices calling for such reforms and urging Africa to stay the course, including advocates for Pan-Africanism such as the late Tajudeen Abdul Raheem, Adebayo Olukoshi, Thandika Mkandawire and Issa Shivji, and institutions such as CODESRIA, Third World Network-Africa and Pambazuka.

Catalysing agency for democracy and inclusive socio-economic systems

We have noted that although the continent is culturally diverse there is a deep-rooted philosophy of community and solidarity which plays a very important role in the organisation of rural production, determining access to natural resources, welfare and the establishment of checks and balances to avoid the excesses of power. At the centre of this framework is the element of local collective agency and solidarity, referred to as *Vuk'uzenzele* ('wake up and do it for yourself') in southern Africa and as *Harambee* in Kenya and *Ujamaa* in Tanzania. These are an approximation of modern day civil society or civic engagement. Aina and Moyo

---

3   TrustAfrica (2006) 'Catalysing African Agency: A Strategic Plan'. Unpublished.

(2013) provide a continent-wide analysis of these forms of solidarity as the bedrock of what we are referring to as the endogenous norms of African philanthropy. Furthermore, African society is dominated by associational activities – in many cases these forms of solidarity have been replicated in urban areas through formations such as burial societies, savings clubs, and associational activities within religious groups whose main purpose revolves around promoting solidarity and collective economic agency. Whilst we acknowledged the global nomenclature on civil society we also pursued any Africanist appreciation of the meaning of civil society not only as a site of contesting and mediating the influence of power but as one of organic solidarity and collective agency. Our approach has entailed nurturing and strengthening associational life as we believe that it is an integral pillar of democratic governance. We have also worked tirelessly on broadening the meaning of democracy beyond civil and political rights and freedoms to economic, social and cultural rights and indeed into social justice. Our concept of democracy includes freedoms from repression, conflict, vulnerability, hunger, disease and ignorance.

Our partnerships on the continent

From the beginning we appreciated that there was no way we could address the continent's most pressing challenges without working with others. We have since then positioned ourselves as a facilitator of processes of change on the continent. We view ourselves as a credible landscape interpreter and an honest broker responsible for helping forge alliances. We are also a respected convener, providing space for reflections and learning, and are continuously improving our work collectively and individually as social change agents on the continent. We have mostly worked with civil society partners and university-based researchers; our contact with governments has been very limited. We had a very successful collaboration with the government of Senegal over the hosting of the Higher Education Summit and have worked with a number of government-based investment promotion agencies, but we are primarily a civil society focused foundation.

When we began operations, civil society organisations in our target areas were, for the most part, relatively nascent and had few or no platforms for networking and collective action. We were very clear from the onset that we would be focusing on ensuring policy improvements to achieve the twin goals of democracy and development. We further made a commitment to consult widely through convenings and scoping studies that we would commission. In many instances these convenings provided an opportunity for the development of broadly shared agendas as well as the development of loose networks with the capacity to raise resources beyond the initial funding from TrustAfrica.

It is important to note that in many instances our partners face an existential threat at two levels, namely financial sustainability and shrinking public spaces (Moyo, 2011). Our partners have had to constantly navigate between dealing with resource limitations and threats to their personal freedoms, and in some cases the closure of their organisations due to changes in the operating environment; for instance, in many countries governments are considering a cap on how much of an institution's budget can be funded from outside. At times donor interests shift, further deepening the challenge to organisations depending on a single funder. We have occasionally had to provide emergency grants to help some of our human rights partners to move to into safety in the face of threats from state agents. We have also come to celebrate the creative ways in which our partners have leveraged the small grants we have advanced them to unlock more resources. For instance, in 2011 we gave a small grant to an association of smallholders in east and southern Africa and they used it for convenings with parliamentary committees on agriculture. In the process their efforts caught the attention of a bigger donor who then gave them a grant of €1.8 million to carry out similar work in the region. Our role has always been to go beyond simply issuing a grant; we walk with partners through processes of co-creation, and have been amazed at how some of our partners have reciprocated by opening doors for us in spaces where we had not made inroads. In relation to our illicit financial flows work, for example, our initial partnership with the Southern Africa Trust (SAT) has evolved into assisting the Southern Africa Development Community (SADC) to develop a strategy on domestic resource mobilisation, which in turn has ensured that illicit financial flows are part of the sub-region's development agenda.

In 2011 we began an initiative aimed at ensuring that the reduction of crimes of impunity was prioritised and that the perpetrators of political violence be brought to book.[4] Initially we were criticised for being pro-ICC but I am glad to note that, together with our partners working in Uganda, Kenya and Ivory Coast, we have managed to turn the debate to focus on victims' rights and are beginning to see policy traction in those

---

4   See Sipalla in this volume.

countries. The recent trial of Hissène Habré here in Dakar, which we fully endorse, will hopefully contribute towards increased confidence in the administration of justice through African institutions. The emerging consensus on illicit financial flows as one of the biggest drivers of social and economic injustice also derives from the groundbreaking work of our partners. When we ventured into the arena of fighting against illicit financial flows in 2013, to the best of our knowledge there were very few African groups working on this issue and there was no significant pan-African network dedicated to the it. We give credit to our partners who have made sure that most domestic resource mobilisation processes now officially recognise IFFs as an issue requiring urgent attention.[5] The majority of the changes we are seeing in areas such as smallholder agriculture in Ghana and Malawi are due to the work of our partners who have gone beyond the call of duty to ensure that governments remain accountable to their citizens.[6]

However, this journey has not been without challenges. One of the early observations that we made had to do with what I call the 'myth of civil society in Africa'. There are many reasons why civil society cannot address all of the continent's problems.

First, there is an inadequate and uneven supply of CSOs across the continent. We have found that anglophone countries tend to have stronger CSOs than francophone countries. Interestingly, francophone countries tend to produce strong social movements that are not necessarily supported by philanthropy, raising questions about whether philanthropy captures, modifies or even distorts actors such as social movements.[7]

Second, local non-state policy research capacity has not yet had any significant impact on policymaking. Full use is not being made of research findings generated in Africa when decision makers formulate policies (Ajakaiye, 2007: 19). Governments' policy making processes are currently ad hoc in nature, and are often driven by either political or donor interests.

Third, we have come to realise that civil society responses to government's weak policies can at times be also inadequate, very formulaic and, quite frankly, at times do not create viable alternatives. The continent has gone through campaigns for budget literacy, especially

---

5   See Ngirande in this volume.
6   See Mubaya in this volume.
7   This is a critical organising question which is perhaps best discussed within the emergent discourse on organic vs. artificial civil societies.

with women's lobby groups demanding gender sensitive budgets. This was followed by the 'percentage' movement: 15% for education, 10% for agriculture, etc. In the meantime, Africa was losing close to $60 billion annually through illicit financial flows and very few in civil society were addressing this problem. In countries such as Malawi, Lesotho and Tanzania – because of their significant dependence on direct budgetary support – we were uncritically swallowing donor prescriptions.

Fourth, despite the evident systemic and structural causes of most of the problems that Africa faces, most of civil society was working in rigid silos. These developed around how organisations positioned themselves and were perceived; also – widely acknowledged but not openly discussed – competition for donor funding has discouraged a more collective approach to solving issues. There were, and still are, many layers of silos, starting with those established by thematic areas of work, such as a focus on one set of rights vis-à-vis another. There are divisions between policy reform/advocacy and service delivery; between think tanks and advocates of change. There are silos with a regional focus and those with a national focus. The list goes on. These silos are not natural, but over time they have become a normal way of organising within the formal civic space. The more professional the space becomes, the more silos we will see. These silos unfortunately limit the manner in which we frame or understand a public problem and also how we consequently conceive and craft solutions and harness collective action. They eventually create privileged islands in a sea of poverty and injustice. The World Social Forum and various sub-regional forums attempted to break the silos by bringing together actors focused on progressive social change into a single conversation, but the energy in this space has also waned considerably.

Fifth, the connection between partner organisations and the communities that they serve is limited. The era of the concerned community organiser starting a movement around an issue such as safer streets for girls is slowly being replaced by the more sophisticated approach that starts off with offices before creating a credible connection with the community. In fact, community based organisations have rarely featured as a significant constituency of philanthropy's grant-making process – perhaps because we are pitching change at a policy level which requires certain expert skills.

Addressing supply-side challenges: The promise of African philanthropy

African philanthropy is best captured when understood as a form of agency, especially in a context where the dominant narratives were of an Africa that was conflict-ridden and hopeless. We felt the need to force-fully display African agency, and our knowledge products and platforms contributed towards the repositioning of Africa as an engaged continent. A major focus of TrustAfrica's work over the past ten years was on grow-ing the field of African philanthropy.[8] Our energies have been devoted towards producing knowledge that affirms the historical and culturally embedded forms of giving popular across Africa. We have produced a volume of essays[9] on the subject and contributed book chapters, jour-nal papers and conference papers. We have also, working together with others such as Southern Africa Trust, Kenya Community Development Fund and AWDF, led the process of establishing the Africa Philanthropy Network (initially called the African Grantmakers Network) and partic-ipated in many forums focused on advancing the practice of what we loosely referred to as African philanthropy. There are two broad ten-dencies within African philanthropy; one is largely horizontal and spon-taneous and can be called peer-to-peer giving;[10] the other attempts to replicate global practices of the high net worth individuals who establish formal vehicles to give away some of their wealth to causes they identify with. Our approach has not been to seek to replace one with the other but to find ways in which both global and African philanthropy can co-exist and create synergies where necessary.

We have faced a number of challenges in our efforts to nurture and stimulate African philanthropy. For instance, we are yet to raise any meaningful resources from Africa-based philanthropists despite the increased giving from this group. The shortage of local funding, and the consequent reliance on the global north, inevitably raises question, about the authenticity of African foundations. However, evidence from Aina and Moyo (2013) shows that even with funds from global philan-thropies, a foundation rooted on the continent and well grounded with local communities can add enormous value to development processes. In a recently completed performance review of TrustAfrica, it was noted

---

8   See Moyo in this volume.
9   See Aina and Moyo, 2013.
10   Wilkinson-Maposa et al. (2013).

that we face the risk of being seen as pushing a foreign agenda on the continent because of our reliance on non-African resources. This is a challenge that many organisations face. Indeed, reliance on non-African resources has been used in attempts to delegitimise civil society work that makes the state uncomfortable, such as the promotion of democracy and good governance, accountability and transparency. In Kenya and Zimbabwe, for instance, our work against impunity has been challenged as part of broader 'regime plots' orchestrated by imperial forces, in the process forcing us into a defensive position.

There are a number of reasons that may explain why African philanthropy is yet to play a significant role. First, the Africa Rising narrative that is feeding the assumptions about the growth of the middle class, and especially of the high net worth individuals (HNWIs), may be more of an ephemeral moment than a sustained process of growth. The president of the Ford Foundation rightly observed that the basis of most American philanthropic foundations is a well-functioning market economy. African approaches to economic liberalisation have rarely focused on developing a national entrepreneurial class, rather they have focused on opening their economies up for foreign direct investment, which is usually driven by multinational corporations whose contribution to philanthropy on the continent is insignificant. As a consequence, Africa has not seen the emergence of a broader entrepreneurial class as seen in Malaysia, South Korea and China.

Second, although there is recognition of the importance of philanthropy, very few national governments have taken steps to create an enabling environment by providing tax incentives, or easing registration requirements. A study carried out by the Southern Africa Trust in seven southern African countries found that outside South Africa there is no tax incentive for giving. However, evidence from TrustAfrica and UBS research suggests that tax and other conducive regulatory environments are not currently a key driver or incentive to many existing HNWIs (Mahomed et al., 2014).

Third, the platforms for creating a community of practice amongst HNWI foundations remain limited. Conversations on how to give, where to give and who to work with either do not exist or have very narrow outreach. The need for such platforms becomes even more critical in light of the fact that many HNW philanthropists have preferred to keep their giving decisions internal. While the benefits of such fora have not been adequately understood by HNW philanthropists, these challenges could also be due to the infrastructure sector not having determined how to get the attention of HNW philanthropists to engage more with them.

Giving by Africa's HNWI remains largely untracked, but for the most part it focuses on addressing the symptoms and not the underlying causes of inequality. While there are certainly exceptions to this, and these exceptions are slowly increasing, many of the African HNWI foundations are focused on issues such as scholarships for under-privileged children, access to medical care, feeding schemes and relief in times of disasters. Others are engaged in infrastructure projects. However noble these causes, they do not address the underlying systemic causes of inequality and poverty. Furthermore, there is a worrisome trend of Africans giving to universities within the global north and not to those in Africa or the global South. For instance, a Nigerian billionaire, Mohammed Indinmi, donated $14 million to Lynn University in Florida.[11]

The promise of African agency

Ultimately, agency lies with the citizens, and institutions like ours can only contribute to strengthening what already exists. We have always looked at African agency as made up of two pillars, philanthropy and civil society. We have reason to believe that the next ten years will be a period of consolidation in both. Despite the prevailing less-than-satisfactory state of African philanthropy, we still view it as an important development that requires careful and committed nurturing. We have seen a slow but exciting growth of Africans giving to important causes and we are in a period of maturation of CSOs making important contributions towards the deepening of democratic practice and the achievement of social and economic justice. The active contribution to national and regional policy processes has begun to bear fruit in terms of policy realignment and state delivery.

The potential of African philanthropy

There is a growing recognition of the role that philanthropy can play in Africa's quest for equitable and democratic transformation. In the past decades, many have viewed philanthropy as a type of aid, a form of support from outside the continent. To be sure, the story of Africa's liberation and even early post-independence development initiatives

---

11   http://nigerianuniversityscholarships.com/nigerian-billionaire-donates-4-2-billion-naira-american-university/

would have been very different if it were not for the investments made by philanthropic foundations based abroad. However, there is a new excitement in the continent, centred on the possibilities of the contribution of home-grown philanthropy. Many important strategy documents have considered the key role that philanthropy can play, at continental level in the AU's Agenda 2063, in the regional SADC Industrialisation Strategy and Roadmap 2015-2063 and in national level strategies such as in Rwanda.[12]

The growing importance of African philanthropy is grounded in the emerging breed of entrepreneurs, a significant number of whom are committed to the continent's development. The number of dollar millionaires rose from around 130,000 in 2013 (Mahomed et al. 2013), to 165,000 in 2016.[13] These millionaires established more foundations across the continent during this period than ever before, and have made significant philanthropy investments in the areas of health, education, entrepreneurial development and infrastructure improvements (ibid.).

Despite the mounting interest in African philanthropy, we remain very cautious for a number of reasons. In addition to the issues raised in the previous section, we are yet to see the foundations established by the HNWIs being independently run and setting up an endowment for perpetual existence like their northern counterparts. Further, these foundations are yet to provide support in a manner that demonstrates a reduced contribution from the global north. It is ironic that even TrustAfrica, which was established to cultivate the practice of African philanthropy and agency, still finds itself dependent on northern donors.

The potential of civil society

We have witnessed a commendable growth of CSOs that are driving pro-poor policy positions. These have varying capacities in terms of framing policy options, generating datasets to justify policy positions or to evaluate impact, and advocating for policy reforms. However, the proliferation of such organisations with policy research capacity has not yet had a significant impact overall on policymaking, especially in terms of opening the process and improving the content of those policies. However, we have reason to believe that the trend is changing. In the past few years we have seen the AU and a number of African govern-

---

12   See Moyo in this volume.

13   http://www.researchandmarkets.com/reports/3632320/the-africa-2016-wealth-report

ments beginning to implement recommendations made by CSOs, such as the adoption of the Africa Mining Vision (AMV).

As already mentioned, some of the dominant actors within civil society are not sufficiently linked to the grassroots and may not adequately nurture active citizenship. One of the most significant challenges to democratisation is that the most citizens feel powerless, or do not see the need to participate in national processes of electing leaders or exercising control over their communities' and national futures. Levels of voter apathy in national and local government elections have been on the rise since the 1990s. The dominant approaches in electoral democracies have created a schism between the rulers and the ruled. The rulers have over the years either made concessions on what citizens can do or have curtailed processes of broader citizen mobilisation. This has created an environment of uncertainty about what is permissible. We need to take advantage of various AU protocols aimed at enhancing citizen participation in national political processes, regardless of class, race and gender.

Human and political life happens within local communities, and democracy can and should be nurtured at this level. Furthermore, the re-imagining of the public space should include a new understanding of democracy itself in order to capture what others such as Mkandawire (2001, 2011) have called developmental democracy. Developmental democracy acknowledges the importance of civil and political rights and freedoms, but also accords equal weight to the socio-economic imperatives for equitable development within the country. Such a position can potentially lead to a more comprehensive political contract between the governors and the governed. It also raises the bar of performance amongst public officials.

It is worth reiterating that transforming the state as well as strengthening civil society cannot be fully accomplished in the absence of fostering a culture of responsible citizenry, which feeds both civil society as well as the governmental and political process (Daubon, 2007). While some citizens can respond individually to changes in economic conditions, in many instances of cooperation the effect of their collective action is greater than the sum of the different parts.

Furthermore, we note that participation in political processes has often been reduced to tokenism, with functionaries ticking a box to indicate that they have 'engaged' with a community before embarking on a public programme. The limited participation of previously marginalised groups such as women and youths has been identified as inhibiting the potential benefits of a thriving democracy. Many countries have begun to embrace women's participation in politics, but they still remain under-represented. The youth on the other hand are restricted by constitutional provisions that have set age limits on who can participate. We need to broaden participation in politics beyond periodic elections, being in parliament and the capture of state power; instead, we need to position it as a value that every citizen needs to embrace. Democracy is only meaningful when it is substantive, inclusive and responsive to the people's needs.

The challenge that Africa faces is to rethink our politics as everyday interactions that can only be enhanced by the provision of effective platforms for inclusive citizen participation. The prevailing system of periodic elections needs to be complemented by an engaged citizenry that is meaningfully consulted and given appropriate spaces to deliberate on public affairs. An inclusive and participatory government framework, from the local to national levels, is central to this process. Local government is especially important in rural areas where the despotism of traditional authority and the ineffective post-independence decentralised structures have only served to further marginalise rural communities.

Conclusion

Beyond boundaries: Fostering collaboration

Our ten years of working on the continent have taught us a number of things which will not only help us sharpen our way of doing things but will also influence the sector as a whole. Some of the criticisms of our work have to do with a failure to provide long-term funding and an inability to include marginalised voices. The lack of a gender specific lens has also been raised as a weakness.

We take pride in being a learning organisation, and most of the measures that we have taken to reorganise ourselves have been based on such open reflections. Some of the issues that we are perhaps guilty of have to do with our position within the philanthropy chain: at the beginning we were meant to be an autonomous foundation, but we subsequently found ourselves at the mercies of the bigger global foundations and the methods of support that they use, such as project based funding. We, together with others, were established to resolve identifiable issues that are public in nature and the deployment of carefully designed interventions should ideally lead to resolution of the problem.

However, we were also alert to the complexity and inter-connectedness of the problems that the continent has to address, and mid-way through the first decade – after realising the futility of a large portfolio made up mostly of very small grants – we made a decision to support fewer organisations but with significantly larger grants. Furthermore, we encouraged our partners to work within collaborative networks and advocacy movements. Our approach is based on a strong conviction that whilst agency is the fuel, the vehicle that will deliver on the aspirations for a more just order is a developmental and democratic African state.

We see civil society based organisations as the arena of change where history will eventually be made, but we do not claim to have all the solutions. We realise the current limitations within the philanthropy sector, but we are not overwhelmed. Inasmuch as we have realised the need for collaboration amongst CSOs we also see the need for it amongst like-minded philanthropy institutions. We are wary of a grants only approach and are positioning ourselves as an organisation that spans boundaries. Collaboration amongst philanthropy institutions is very limited, but the islands of best practice feature those that are focused on experience sharing. Since 2009 we have managed three donor collaborations, on international criminal justice, anti-corruption in Nigeria and democracy in Zimbabwe. There is reason to believe that such approaches, if properly constituted with clear operating procedures, may have a bigger impact on the systemic issues we are trying to address. Whilst these collaborations have been relatively easy because they are single-issue focused, we hope to establish more sophisticated models addressing matters such as socio-economic justice, education, health and employment. We have devised a more comprehensive suite of tools that we refer to as 'beyond grants', and we will deploy these to ensure that we are enhancing the capacities of civil society organisations as frontline actors of change for social, economic and political justice. Our goal is to break the current false division between funders and develop a community of collaborative changemakers. We are conscious that the agenda described above could be too big for one institution and so we see the need to work towards the creation of sustainable collaborations that will yield the synergies necessary to address the systemic challenges faced by the continent.

References

Aina, T.A. and B. Moyo (2013) *Giving to Help, Helping to Give: The Context and Politics of African Philanthropy*. Dakar, Amalion Publishing.

Ajakaiye, O. (2007) 'Levelling the Playing Field – Strengthening the Role of African Research in Policy-Making in and for Sub-Saharan Africa', in E.T. Ayuk and M.A. Marouani (eds), *The Policy Paradox in Africa: Strengthening Links Between Economic Research and Policymaking*. Trenton, NJ, Africa World Press.

Daubon. R.E. (2007) 'A Civil Investing Strategy for Putting Communities in Charge'. Washington, DC, Kettering Foundation.

Mahomed, H., L.A. Julien and S. Samuels (2014) 'Africa's Wealthy Give Back: A Perspective on philanthropic giving by wealthy Africans in sub-Saharan Africa, with a focus on Kenya, Nigeria and South Africa'. Zurich and Dakar, UBS and TrustAfrica.

Mkandawire, T. (2001) 'Thinking About Developmental States in Africa', *Cambridge Journal of Economics*, 25(3), pp. 289-313.

Mkandawire, T. (2011) 'Rethinking Pan-Africanism, Nationalism and the New Regionalism', in S. Moyo and P.Yeros (eds) 'Reclaiming the Nation: The Return of the National Question in Africa, Asia and Latin America'. New York, Pluto Press

Moyo, B. (ed.) (2010) *(Dis)enabling the Public Sphere: Civil Society Regulation in Africa* (Vol. 1). Midrand, Southern Africa Trust and TrustAfrica.

Wilkinson-Maposa, S., A. Fowler, C. Oliver-Evans and C.F.N. Mulenga (2004). *The Poor Philanthropist: How and why the poor help each other*. Cape Town, University of Cape Town Press.

Printed in the United States
By Bookmasters